I0450701

Toxic Attention

Also by Dr. Sherry L. Meinberg:

The Bogeyman:
Stalking and its Aftermath

Be the Boss of Your Brain:
Take Control of Your Life

Into the Hornet's Nest: An Incredible Look
at Life in an Inner City School

Toxic Attention

Keeping Safe From Stalkers, Abusers, and Intruders

Dr. Sherry L. Meinberg

iUniverse, Inc.
New York Lincoln Shanghai

Toxic Attention
Keeping Safe From Stalkers, Abusers, and Intruders

All Rights Reserved © 2003 by Dr. Sherry L. Meinberg

No part of this book may be reproduced or transmitted in any form or by any means, graphic, electronic, or mechanical, including photocopying, recording, taping, or by any information storage retrieval system, without the written permission of the publisher.

iUniverse, Inc.

For information address:
iUniverse
2021 Pine Lake Road, Suite 100
Lincoln, NE 68512
www.iuniverse.com

ISBN: 0-595-28879-0 (Pbk)
ISBN: 0-595-74901-1 (Cloth)

Printed in the United States of America

This manual is designed to educate; to provide basic information about the subject of stalking in particular and related crimes in general. It is not meant to present all the information available regarding stalkers, abusers, intruders, or their victims, nor is it meant to be legal advice. It was written simply to provide you with an overview, and present suggestions and preventative measures for those who may be on the receiving end of such behavior. The checklists are to be used as a springboard for learning, to complement, amplify, and supplement other books, articles, and organizational input. *Toxic Attention* should be used only as a general guide, since it is based upon the personal experiences of the author, and your experience may differ. It is not meant to replace the advice of trained professionals. Neither the author nor the publisher is engaged in rendering legal, economic, security, self-defense, physical, or psychological services; and shall have neither responsibility nor liability to any person or entity with respect to any damage or loss caused or alleged to be caused directly or indirectly by the information herein. Make intelligent choices, applying only those ideas, procedures, or suggestions that appeal to you, and resonate with your particular situation. Please note the publishing date, as research is still in its infancy, and subject to change. Be aware that laws differ from state to state, regarding the definition of a stalker, as well as victim's rights. If you require in-depth information or additional support services, visit your local bookstores and libraries, consult with experts in the field, check out the internet, continue to monitor films, radio, and news reports, and read various books written about stalking and related crimes, in an effort to keep abreast of new ideas and research.

It is the friends you can
call up at 4 A.M. that matter.
—Marlene Dietrich

DEDICATION

A special thanks, with love, to the women who
were my friends, supporters, and true-blue buds,
who lent me their ears, over lo these many years.
Your caring, thoughtful conversation and laughter
were my lifeline to sanity, and made it all
worthwhile. Hugs and kisses.

Sherry / Terrell / Virginia / Peggy / Martha / Carol

Kathy / Marlene / Geneva / Di / Esther

Mary / Pat / Linda / Mary Val

Jackie / Beth / Betty

Danielle

Maria

Laureen / Sue / Jan

Cecilia / Emmy / Rachel

Donna / Bobbi / Linda / Diane / Vicki

Audrey / Mary Lou / Cheryl / Barbara / Roberta

ACKNOWLEDGMENT

A special thanks is given to Barbara Kaye Cooper for her computer wizardry.

CONTENTS

FOREWORD

It used to be a problem people couldn't talk about easily, because there were no words adequate to describe what was going on. Even the term "stalking" only gradually became the chosen way to describe the behavior. Now, thanks to more than a decade of legislation, every state has a law against stalking, many people know what it is, and victims of this heinous crime are learning to speak out about it to get the help they need.

Stalking is a large problem. According to a national survey conducted by the National Institute of Justice, roughly one million American women and 400,000 American men in the United States are stalked every year. This definition of stalking used here is "a pattern of repeated, unwanted attention, harassment, and contact," which includes such things as following, making harassing phone calls, sending emails, sending "gifts", damaging property, making threats, identity theft, assault, rape, or murder. The NIJ estimates that more than eight million women (8 percent) and two million men (2 percent) in the U.S. will be stalked sometime during their lives.

Stalking is a long-term problem. The average stalking situation lasts for about a year. Most non-stalking crimes are over with quickly, so victims can immediately begin to think of themselves as survivors. People being stalked, however, can never be sure that it is over, because a break of a few weeks or months may be followed by renewed, or even increased, activity by the stalker.

Stalking is a dangerous problem. About one-third of stalking situations involve some type of violence. One study has shown that 8 percent of stalkers either murder their targets, attempt to kill them, or solicit someone to do the killing for them! Domestic violence survivors who are leaving their abusers are at the highest risk, but for other types of stalkers, the longer they stalk, the more dangerous they become.

Stalking causes stress-related problems. The unrelenting stress of being harassed, never knowing what the stalker may do next, can cause a wide range of reaction, ranging from depression, social isolation, sleep disturbance, and hyper-vigilance to the constellation of symptoms that make up Post Traumatic Stress Disorder (PTSD).

Don't think that being stalked is hopeless. The only way to solve a problem is to realistically recognize the problem and take actions that experience has taught can be effective.

Many people move from one place to another in an attempt to get away from their tormentors. That's an expensive and time-consuming thing to do, and isn't necessary in all cases. What is truly said is a situation where someone moves, perhaps several times, and the stalker manages to follow. That can be prevented, with adequate advance planning.

Some police departments have come a long way in the last few years in dealing appropriately with stalking. People who are stalked in their jurisdictions have the luxury of knowing that their concerns are being taken seriously. Some police departments are still in the dark ages and victims in their territories quickly learn that they cannot depend on the police for help, and thus are very much on their own when it comes to taking protective action.

Dr. Sherry L. Meinberg's *Toxic Attention: Keeping Safe from Stalkers, Abusers, and Intruders* provides two things that people need who are suffering through this kind of relentless pursuit—the tools to help them to become responsible for their own safety, and empathy for the emotional toll this crime inflicts.

It lists hundreds of detailed actions that substantially increase one's margin of safety, interspersed with real case studies (her own and others) that generously illustrate the points made. Sherry Meinberg should know, as the person in the U.S. who has been stalked the longest, over four decades, and who has made a research study of this topic, what works and what doesn't.

If you are being stalked, harassed, threatened, or abused, this book will help you to take back control of your life. Nothing removes fear like the confidence that comes from knowing you are prepared to meet the future on your terms, not your stalker's.

The power is yours. You just have to learn how to use it.

—Lyn Bates

Lyn Bates is the Vice President of AWARE (Arming Women Against Rape and Endangerment, www.aware.org), a nonprofit organization that provides information and training to enable women to avoid, deter, repel or resist crimes ranging from minor harassment to violent assault. She is the author of *Safety for Stalking Victims* (iUniverse Press, 2001), a book for people who were told to "Be careful," without being told precisely *how* to be careful. She is a contributing editor to *Women&Guns* magazine on topics related to defensive strategies. She is certified to teach a wide range of self-defense techniques, and counsels stalking victims (and those who help them) in areas such as situation analysis, risk assessment, and the development of detailed, highly personalized self-protection plans.

I use not only all the brains I have,
but all I can borrow.
—Woodrow Wilson

INTRODUCTION

According to the FBI, I have the dubious honor of being the longest-stalked person in the nation: four decades, and counting. My personal story was chronicled in *The Bogeyman: Stalking and its Aftermath* (iUniverse, 2003, ISBN 0-595-26271-6), and this companion manual is a direct result of readers' requests for more safety suggestions. Over the years, everyone warned me to "Be careful," but no one ever gave me specifics as to *how* to manage that. As such, I learned everything about being a survivor in a trial-and-error fashion, emphasis on the error. Most of my survival education has come in the proverbial hard way, through making a thousand and one painful mistakes. My hit-or-miss method resulted from having no road map to follow; from having received no input from books, magazines, speeches, or films, and with no outside help from individuals or organizations. After all, the word *stalker* hadn't yet been coined in the sixties.

I am now a reluctant expert on the subject. Know at the outset that this is not my chosen field or area of qualification. I am not formally educated in either the clinical or forensics professions, nor the field of police science. I am, however, qualified to give advice and counsel, simply by virtue of my experience; by having been on the receiving end of stalking behavior for two-thirds of my lifetime. As a result, I have some words of hard-won wisdom and advice on the subject.

Although predatory behavior has historically been recognized since the dawn of time, stalking has only recently been recognized as a crime. It is clearly on the rise worldwide, and has swelled to plague proportions throughout the country (over one and a half million adults are stalked annually in the USA). After years of working with stalking victims on a one-to-one basis, I came to the conclusion that through recording my own stalking experiences and observations, I would be able to serve a wider audience in the same amount of time.

Understand that the following information is not new, by any means (numerous tip sheets are available through various local groups, national organizations, and the Internet), and much is simply common sense. Upon reading the latest stalking research, I would always nod and say, "Uh-huh, I did that," or "Yes!" or "Nope, that didn't work for me." So all these years later, experts are saying many of the same things that I figured out on my own, and had actually put into practice, over a forty-year period.

The information and suggestions in this manual have been placed for fast and easy reference. Section I—the Stalker's Profile and the Personal Applications—is presented in butterfly form. It provides over fifty ways to recognize a potential stalker or domestic abuser, as well as methods to effectively deal with particular items relating to a stalker's or abuser's behavior. It is designed to be read across the two pages, so reading (5) under the Stalker's Profile corresponds to (5) under Personal Applications, as in, "Here are the facts, and here's what you can do about it." Section II offers practical tools to take care of yourself, when dealing with a stalker, abuser, or intruder. It is simply a series of check-off lists, with advice and recommendations regarding specific safety concerns (personal, family, home, social, travel, work, and support services), as well as health issues (physical, mental, emotional, and recovery). Think of this section as a plan, a map, a guide, or a recipe for general safety. Section III presents current California stalking laws that may help in your situation, as well as a selected bibliography of resource material, and related web sites and links.

Some of the listed preventative measures may seem to be more extreme than others. Utilize only those that you feel comfortable with, and that apply to your specific situation and income. The lines are printed for you to easily keep track of your response to the ideas: Simply place a check mark by those items that you have achieved or put into motion. Place an X next to those ideas that do not pertain to your situation, or do not appeal to you, so you needn't bother with them again. And leave blank those suggestions that you are working on, or may return to later, if the situation changes.

Understand that the prolonged, high-level stress resulting from stalkers, abusers, or intruders, can profoundly disturb your physical, mental, and emotional health. By utilizing many of the suggestions in this manual, you will significantly reduce or deter your chances of becoming a victim of their violence. And, since you won't be wasting precious time reinventing the wheel, you can use your brain power to help yourself in other ways. Taking control of your safety is critical. Devise a practical plan that works for you. Take action. NOW.

PART I

STALKER AND VICTIM INFORMATION

STALKER'S PROFILE

Check out these characteristics and warning signs of a potential stalker:

(1) Experts at camouflage, stalkers appear to be conventional in appearance; just a regular Joe, not commanding much attention. Clean-cut, they are often excessively neat, and present a calm or quiet exterior. They are extremely cooperative and well-mannered, easily blending in with the crowd, although they are not part of any group. Displaying an appealing facade, they appear to be normal, average, ordinary citizens.

(2) Research suggests that most stalkers are older and smarter, or at least more educated, than other types of offenders. The majority of stalkers are male, with the overwhelming majority of victims being female.

(3) Stalkers have numerous similarities. Even so, they are a diverse group, drawn from all ethnic, social, and economic backgrounds, with a wide variety of histories, behaviors, and mental disorders. There is no single "one size fits all" profile. Stalkers display a broad range of motivations, behaviors, and traits, producing a wide variety of strange incidents.

(4) Stalkers generally prey upon those who are attractive and appealing, or friendly and outgoing; the approachable, girl/boy-next-door type. Victims frequently possess a higher educational background, social standing, or economic level than that of the stalker. Often, those in the helping professions are targeted, because of their warmth and caring concern for others. Less often, victims include those of celebrity status.

(5) The most common form of stalking (well over half) involves those who have dated or been sexually intimate in the past. These stalkers simply refuse to let go. Less often, acquaintances, former bosses, and even complete strangers, are targeted. A point to consider: the less of an actual relationship, the more mentally disturbed the stalker.

(6) Lacking a core identity, the stalker forms an adolescent attachment—a fantasy of magical, pure, or untainted love—with the target. Admiration and idealization is in operation, as he/she sets the object of desire on a pedestal. Worshiping this chosen one, the stalker sees the victim as the *only* person who can fill the void and make things turn out right (a sort of savior figure), or make things better (a Rock of Gibraltar role). Preoccupied with the target, reality and fantasy become confused in the stalker's mind, linking the two together forever.

PERSONAL APPLICATIONS

Before becoming involved in a new relationship, or when involved in an abusive situation, consider the following safety measures:

(1) Learn not to be deceived by mere appearances or your own projections. Do not be fooled by a person's conventional looks, appealing manner, and traditional clothes. Pay less attention to what that person says, than to what he/she *does*. Be aware; be awake to each experience. Stop, look, listen, and *feel*. Keep your eyes as wide open as your heart.

(2) Keep in mind that just because a person is older doesn't mean that he/she is more mature. And being a tad smarter only means that a stalker can be more persuasive, manipulative, and resourceful in his/her pursuit activities. Do not underestimate a stalker.

(3) Do not expect a single description of stalkers, as their behavior can manifest in limitless ways. There is a remarkable variety in their actions. Your particular experiences may not match the literature (some of mine were different). Look for the overarching pattern of pursuit.

(4) There are no boundaries—racial, ethnic, religious, or socioeconomic—when it comes to stalking victims. (One man I know was stalked by his own father for a three-year period. The behavior only ceased when the father died.) Anyone, regardless of age and gender, can become a target. Most victims are ordinary citizens.

(5) There is not much you can do to counteract this item, since a relationship between the two of you may have been long over, or was only a figment of the stalker's imagination to begin with. Simply bumping into someone at a store, or an off-hand comment, or a meaningless facial or body gesture, could cement a fixation.

(6) Know up front that you can't change a stalker's mind. You have no control over his/her fantasy life. Never try to argue delusions with a delusional. Understand that you can't communicate *anything* to a stalker that will be understood in the way that you mean it. So save your breath. Attempting to reason with a stalker is an act of utter futility.

(7) A stalker's smiles are counterfeit: measured, calculated, and deceptive; used as a disguise to mask his/her emotions.

(8) With a pleasing manner, a stalker appears to be nice and sincere. He/she uses charm and offers of unsolicited help as hooks, in order to appear normal and be accepted.

(9) In an effort to hide or repress what others may see, a stalker is an expert at mirroring. Agreeing with everything the victim says—in the manner of a chameleon—he/she will reflect the target's values, morals, and judgments. One never knows a stalker's true colors.

(10) A stalker generally has no other outside interests. He/she is an impostor, presenting a false mirror image regarding particular experiences and interests.

(11) A stalker, suffering from antisocial personality disorders, will often use an alias.

(12) A stalker is persuasive and manipulative. He/she will often operate at a whirlwind pace, trying to pressure the victim into premature involvement or commitment.

(13) A stalker is a loner, with no social life.

(14) Stalkers display no anxiety or nervousness in situations where it is warranted, appearing emotionless and unresponsive, like a cardboard cutout. Often, they become physiologically calmer as they observe violence. Some, however, become more violent themselves.

(15) A stalker will often exude a funeral director seriousness, with a dead-pan, poker face.

(7) Does this person's smile telegraph warmth, sincerity, and acceptance? Or do the smiles seem to be only teeth, manufactured and presented on cue? A genuine smile shows eyes that crinkle or twinkle, not just lips or teeth only. Be conscious of his/her body language and facial expressions, to see whether or not they contradict what is being said. Understand that 86 percent of our communications are nonverbal.

(8) Don't confuse niceness with goodness. Anyone can put up a good front. Stalkers can appear to be the nicest of people until they encounter stress or someone crosses them in some way. Look for chinks in the facade; look behind the social mask. Watch how this person handles *all* emotional states before committing yourself.

(9) If you suspect that this person is mirroring you, ask his/her opinions regarding personal values and social issues *before* you reveal your own. Slide your questions in separately, one by one. Might the answers given be what he/she thinks you want to hear? What does this person do when you present a differing opinion? Does he/she quickly change positions? Ask about his/her goals and expectations. Do later actions match his/her words?

(10) Is there evidence of anything important in this person's life, other than *you*? Be wary of someone who appears to have *exactly* the same hobbies, pastimes, cares or concerns, as yours. Ask for details concerning such passions. Is there any *excitement* with the delivery?

(11) Do you know this person's full name? Nicknames? Do you know if he/she has ever used another name?

(12) Does this person try to rush you into quick decisions? Has he/she tried to pressure you into exclusivity or an instant engagement? Is he/she vigorously pressing for moving in together or a quickie marriage? Go slowly. What's the rush? Keep your options open.

(13) Does this person always want to go everywhere and do everything with you? Alone? Does he/she appear to have any friends? Specifically ask about friends.

(14) Watch for no response or inappropriate responses. Does he/she show a mannequin-like, expressionless reaction to things that would shock the normal person? Is he/she calm when others are surprised or alarmed?

(15) Understand that the most dangerous people are those whose rage is quiet and cold.

(16) Stalkers do not have a genuine sense of humor.

(17) Stalkers were often mistreated as children, either through neglect, growing up in dangerous situations, watching repeated violent acts (both real and media induced), or receiving severe physical abuse themselves. They come from emotionally barren backgrounds.

(18) Stalkers frequently show signs of trouble—displaying an antisocial streak—at an early age: problems at school, with neighbors, and peers; bullying younger children; playing with matches or outright arson; torturing animals; truancy; running away, et cetera.

(19) Stalkers have had chronic failures in their social and sexual relationships during adolescence and young adulthood.

(20) Overwhelming evidence shows that stalkers are likely to have a history of prior psychiatric difficulties, including depression, disordered thinking, obsessive-compulsive behavior, and paranoid disorders, in addition to their abnormal power and control needs. Anywhere between 50 to 90 percent of stalkers suffer from some sort of mental illness, while the rest are on the far edge of normal.

(21) A stalker has a history of violence, and is indifferent to the pain he/she causes others.

(22) A stalker has a reckless disregard for laws and for safety; the rules don't apply to him/her.

(23) Ample evidence shows that over half of stalkers have prior criminal histories, both related and unrelated to stalking behavior. In most cases, incarceration hasn't helped much, in terms of attitude or behavior. (This doesn't necessarily mean that they were actually jailed for their offenses.)

(24) A stalker will often have long-held hidden resentments, hostilities, and attitudes simmering just below the surface.

(25) A stalker has a need to be right about everything, and is allergic to criticism. Blaming others for problems of his/her own making, there is always a ready excuse. Everyone else is at fault.

(16) Does this person display a sense of humor? (Always, sometimes, never?) When? (Only when you're looking or expecting a certain response?) Does his/her laughter sound sincere? Listen closely.

(17) Carefully consider his/her family members. Explore family trees and connections of compatibility. Know that when you marry, you're marrying history.

(18) Since juvenile records are normally sealed from the public, what do you know about his/her childhood and adolescent years? Are youthful experiences ever even mentioned? Does he/she seem to have a secret childhood? Experts suggest that even if you feel rude or ridiculous, *ask*. If no answers are forthcoming, be willing to *guess*.

(19) Ask about previous boy/girlfriends. Did he/she have *any* long-term, meaningful relationships? If so, find out what happened to end them.

(20) Of course, this person may never have received professional help. If you are not privy to psychologically sensitive information, consider: Does this person experience mood swings, even without the presence of alcohol or drugs? Has he/she taken part in individual or group psychotherapy? Is this person taking medication? What kind? Find out. In the absence of evidence, how does he/she feel about therapy, and mental health professions, in general?

(21) Know that the best predictor of violence is past violence. Check it out.

(22) Does this person seemingly write his/her own rules on a day-to-day basis? Is basic safety not an issue? Does he/she show a disregard for other's safety? (For instance, what have you noticed about his/her driving? Too fast? Cuts in and out of traffic? Stops on a dime? Drives too close to other vehicles for comfort? Won't stop unsafe driving behavior, even when requested to do so?

(23) Does his/her history include police encounters? It would never occur to the average citizen to question a new acquaintance about previous prison offenses (threats, assaults, battery, stalking). Ask anyway. Check it out. In the absence of such detailed information, what is his/her attitude toward the police and the courts?

(24) Be alert to any smoldering resentments, unreasonable ill will, unswerving hostility, or racist attitudes lurking within. Look for his/her Achilles' heel.

(25) No matter how persuasive the argument, don't buy into accepting blame for this person's behavior. Provoking anger in another is entirely different from *causing* the violence. It is not your fault. Self-blame is not helpful.

(26) A stalker is inflexible, resistant to change, and unwilling to compromise.

(27) A stalker often grows up in an addictive home, and may also have a substance abuse problem. The most frequent drugs of abuse or dependence for stalkers include alcohol, marijuana, amphetamines, and cocaine.

(28) A stalker is secretive, deceitful, and often outright lies. He/she will needlessly misinterpret, embellish, grossly distort, and deliberately slant or change the facts to make him/herself look good.

(29) Stalkers show an elevated rate of unemployment *and* underemployment. A strong work ethic is not high on a stalker's list; job-related ambition, accomplishment, and career longevity, is never a goal. Such an individual may have difficulties reacting to normal everyday stress, and may consequently perform poorly, having troubles at his/her place of employment. There are often serious performance issues and/or insubordination incidents on record (purposely causing problems, disruptions, threats, unreasonable grievances, sabotage, as well as problems with authority figures).
(30) Stalkers have inappropriate role models, displaying a fascination or identification with violent people in history, fiction, or the news.

(31) A stalker will often justify the violence of others.

(32) Some stalkers consider guns, knives, blunt instruments, handcuffs, chains, axes, crossbows, and less often, even bombs, as suitable for control or revenge. Their involvement may include buying, selling, carrying, and/or collecting them. Know that weapons represent power, and are seen as ways to control and intimidate. Only as a last resort are such weapons used to wreak revenge.
(33) For the vast majority of stalkers, a history of domestic violence is apparent. It is a prominent theme in a stalker's relationship.

(26) Normal thought is forever being reviewed, recycled, and renewed. Mature minds change when one's perspective shifts. We stretch and expand and grow through adjusting. Does this person appear too set, too rigid, too inflexible?

(27) Have you seen evidence that this person is enamored with alcohol? Or is he/she working up the pharmaceutical ladder, from pot to glue to crystal meth to acid to cocaine to heroin? If not, do his/her posters, clothes, jewelry, or tattoos display such an interest?

(28) If answers to your questions seem to be on the other side of vague, or highly suspect, make the commitment to put forth the effort to get clear, specific, accurate information. By choosing to ignore the facts, you may be putting yourself at risk. Make an informed decision. (Refer to the Internet: **whoishe.com** or **whoisshe.com**, **firstinc.com**, **backgroundchecks.com**, and the like, for a personal profile and background check on an individual. This type of service provides a basic background check, a criminal or civil record check, or a comprehensive background check. Check out other similar services in your area).

(29) Is this person employed? Full time, part time, seasonal, or whenever work is available? Is the employment proportional to the level of his/her ability and/or formal education? In the absence of job information, is an unstable work record demonstrated? Is he/she unreliable, irresponsible, showing poor judgment? Frequently late or absent? Understand that by not working, a stalker has more time for stalking behavior, and then stalking *you* becomes his/her full time quest/fixation/career. Know that joblessness is one of the top ten risk factors for stalkers.

(30) Who are his/her role models? Jack the Ripper, Lizzie Bordon, Hannibal Lecter, Stalin, Hitler, Mao, Pol Pot, and the like, should clearly tip you off. (If your role models are Ghandi, Mother Theresa, Nelson Mandela, and the Dalai Lama, while this person's are Jeffrey Dahmer, Robert Bardo or John Hinckley Jr., you know you do not have a meeting of the minds).

(31) Does this person justify the violence of others—supplying reasons and excuses—whether knowing the perpetrators or not (Bernie Goetz, for instance)?

(32) Do you see evidence of a fascination with weaponry (books, posters, or actual weapons)? Does he/she talk or joke about them, caressing such items, or playing around with them? Are weapons ever displayed in a threatening manner?

(33) Understand that domestic violence is not just a single act. It is a continual pattern of physical, sexual, and psychological abuse. What do you know about his/her previous relationships?

(34) Stalkers have a macho entitlement attitude, acting as if they are absolute monarchs who rule by divine right ("king of the castle," "lord of the manor," "master of his/her domain," "male privilege," "his/her way or the highway"). The victim has no rights.

(35) A stalker refuses to take the word "no" seriously. He/she has a hard time taking "no" for an answer, totally discounting the word; seemingly not hearing it, or downright ignoring it completely. This refusal to accept rejection or abandonment is seen as a way to rewrite his/her childhood. To ensure that history doesn't repeat itself, such behavior turns into dominance.

(36) Stalking behavior builds slowly, with seemingly innocent activities (phone calls, driving by, leaving gifts, sending flowers) that are often seen as flattering at first blush. When the attention becomes unwanted, persistent, and threatening, it should be a clear signal that these are not the actions of a lovelorn suitor, or a simple case of "puppy love," or the result of a broken-heart.

(37) It is difficult for stalkers to tolerate disappointment and frustration, or to control their impulses, becoming angry over real or imagined slings and arrows.

(38) A stalker will often display storm trooper tactics to get his/her way.

(39) Some stalkers are psychopaths, overlooking and overriding other people's feelings and wishes, having no conscience or remorse. They are untroubled by the consequences of their actions.

(40) Some stalkers are paranoid; suspicious and distrustful of others. This type of individual thinks that "everyone" is out to get him/her; that the "world" is conspiring against him/her. This person invests others with the worst possible thoughts and motives, expecting them to lie, cheat, or steal from him/her. A paranoid stalker may think that people are actually plotting to harm him/her in some way. Believing that they themselves are the victims, stalkers are bent on "getting even."

(34) Does this person feel entitled to whatever he/she wants, simply by virtue of being alive (male/bigger/stronger/breadwinner/cultural expectations)? Does this person operate from the mindset that he/she *deserves* what is wanted, with no questions asked? Does he/she demand whatever *when* it is wanted, refusing to delay gratification? Does this person maintain that you belong to him/her? That it is his/her right to deal with you in any manner? Is no discussion allowed, or no backtalk tolerated?

(35) Keep in mind the popular feminist sayings regarding the word: N-O spells "no"; What part of "no" don't you understand? and, "No" is a complete sentence. Refusing to hear the word is a clear signal of trouble. If "no" is disregarded, it is often rationalized away ("Her family made her get the divorce. I know she still loves me"), and becomes a control issue. Experts maintain that you should never relent on this issue."No" means no. Do not vacillate. It you do so, it sets the stage for future control.

(36) The most common form of stalking behaviors is repeated phone calls (unidentified hangups, disguised calls, obscene calls, incessant ringing, and conversational). Calling episodes vary in motivation, intensity, and length. Understand that the unwanted, relentless pursuit by a stalker does not mean that you are special. Persistence does not prove love. It simply proves that the stalker is mentally disturbed. By staying involved with you, in whatever way possible, he/she becomes a consistent part of your life.

(37) Disappointments are a part of life. How does this person deal with them? Do minor molehills and simple inconveniences cascade into major catastrophes? Does he/she break things, throw things, or resort to vandalism? Do you detect an increase in abusive behavior toward inanimate objects?

(38) Does this person resort to shouting, bullying, and physical abuse as a way of handling conflict? Are you hyperalert at responding to his/her facial expressions, body posture, and tone of voice? Do you adapt your behavior to avoid his/her explosions?

(39) Does this person ever extend sympathy? If he/she lacks empathy or concern for the welfare of others, know that *you* will be in that spot sooner or later. Does he/she lack remorse or guilt, seemingly having a black hole for a conscience?

(40) Does this person give credit where credit is due, and offer praise or congratulations? Does he/she express appreciation for anything? Remember that you are a part of "everyone" as well as part of "the world." What will happen when *you* start being seen as the enemy? Know that a merely annoying attraction can morph into a dangerous obsession at any time.

(41) Stalkers often had a chaotic upbringing, which certainly explains their compulsive need to be in charge. When love is missing, a stalker will look for substitutes. To a stalker, being in control is a replacement, or alternative, for love.

(42) Like toddlers, stalkers are territorial: mine, mine, mine.

(43) Stalkers will often follow a victim, watching at a distance.

(44) Stalkers may "coincidentally" be sighted by the victim at public places and events (restaurants, movies, concerts, parks, and dances). On later occasions, the stalker will "accidentally" bump into the victim face-to-face, and attempt conversations.

(45) A stalker is extremely jealous of both the victim's actual and perceived relationships; not just those that are sexual in nature, but the victim's friends, close family members and coworkers, are seen as a threat, as well; anyone, or any pet, that the target spends time with, is seen as competition, and viewed as an adversary.

(46) A stalker is unable to cope with loss or abandonment. He/she can't take rejection, refusing to be ignored, because of the threat to his/her identity.

(47) In an effort to keep the contact open, a stalker will make small, seemingly reasonable requests (asking for a lost phone number or address of someone else, information, *anything* to continue the attachment).

(48) A stalker will use guilt, insults, and all manner of harassment, to provoke a response.

(49) Generalized threats ("You're going to be sorry!"), eventually move into specific threats ("I'm going to get you fired!" or "I'll tell your secrets," or "I'll

(41) Is this person a control freak? Does he/she tell you what to do, what to say, what to wear? Does he/she seek to impose ideas, rules, and choices upon you? Does he/she need to control your activities, purchases, and outside friendships? Does he/she demand that you account for your time in an accusing tone? Know that it isn't love if you can't say what you think and feel.

(42) Does this person have a hard time sharing? (*My* house; *My* car; *My* money; My child)? Does he/she think of you as a possession?

(43) Has this person appeared to shadow you at times? Does there seem to be a systematic surveillance being undertaken?

(44) Has he/she ever unexpectedly appeared at public sites or events that you attend, seemingly by chance? More than once? Has this person shown up at smaller functions, or more private gatherings?

(45) Does he/she display obvious proprietary behavior? Does this person guard you like a rottweiler? Do you feel smothered? Is he/she suspicious of those you spend your time with? Does this person expect you to prove your loyalty by sacrificing all other relationships? Is he/she out to destroy your ties with others? Or suggested moving where you don't know anyone? Does this person expect you to give up your beloved pet(s)? If nothing else, any one of the above serve as a revelation of extreme selfishness, indicating deep emotional problems. Know that possessive attention is not a sign of passionate love. Do not feel flattered or comforted by this excessive interest and domineering behavior. It isn't love when he/she can't give you the freedom to live your own life.

(46) Don't feel sorry for him/her, displaying sympathy; Don't worry about hurting his/her feelings; Don't try to reject the individual by letting him/her down easily. None of that kind of thinking will make a whit of difference, and it just *prolongs* your connection, which is what the stalker craves.

(47) Know that any type of connection—even negative—is seen as *progress* to a stalker. Do not angrily respond, or slam down the receiver. Do not cry or plead. You're dealing with intermittent reinforcement here. Seemingly ignore all the his/her efforts. Avoid any contact whatsoever. Think of your stalker as addicted to the relationship. Cold turkey is the only way to handle a detoxing situation. Show that you mean business.

(48) Once you have stated your objections, in no uncertain terms, there is no further need to talk. Do not keep rehashing your position. Never discuss. Never explain. Never make excuses. Say nothing more. Saying you don't want to talk only proves that you will. Zip your lip.

(49) When threatened, consider the stalker's ability to carry out the threats. Does this person actually seem to be willing to end this relationship, or is

drag your name through the mud!"). If those threats aren't working, another way to force the victim is to threaten friends, and even their own children). It is an effective method.

(50) Understand that this is not a brief encounter; stalking is a long, slow crime. The victim is in it for an extended length of time. Stalking behavior is an excessive preoccupation with a specific individual, taking place over a period of weeks, months, and decades, morning, noon, and night.

(51) The stalking experience is cyclical in nature. Mimicking the cycle of domestic violence, stalking generally has three phases: a tension-building phase (the gradual escalation of indirect contact); then a barrage of verbal abuse, threats, and violence (face-to-face encounters); and finally, after relieving the tension, a tapering off of incidents occurs. This can represent a long period of intermittent contact or no contact whatsoever. Then the cycle begins again.

(52) Refusing to let go, a stalker may attempt to enlist the aide of his/her own relatives. Becoming involved, family members will make phone calls, write letters, assist with surveillance, and generally do anything to help recover the relationship. Some provide assistance because they want to keep the status quo with their basic family unit intact, others buy into the illusion, and others help because they've been given misleading information about the situation.

(53) Sometimes a stalker will even try to become friendly with the victim's friends or family members, to keep tabs on the victim's whereabouts and activities. They can be totally believable and extremely persuasive.

(54) Stalkers will sometimes steal personal items from the victim, or leave unusual items for the victim to find.

(55) Stalkers take no responsibility for their actions. Know that their typical psychological defenses include denial ("I never threatened you! *When* did I ever threaten you?"), minimization ("I was just kidding. You *know* I didn't mean it."), rationalization ("You deserved much more than that!"), and projection of blame upon the victim ("It was consensual. Admit it. You wanted it!").

(56) Many stalkers are schizophrenics. Although they appear psychologically sound, they hold onto totally unsupported fixed beliefs. Schizophrenia is an illness of distorted thought. Schizophrenics have bizarre, completely off-the-wall delusions, hallucinations (both seeing and hearing things that are not there), and disorganized speech. Medication can only control the symptoms, it cannot produce a cure. However, since most schizophrenics don't believe they're sick, they don't seek treatment anyway. Unfortunately, neither prison time nor hospitalization is enough to eradicate their delusions.

he/she only blowing off steam? Do not show fear. Know that the value of a threat is determined by *your* reaction. Experts stress reacting calmly, silently asking yourself, "Am I in danger, right *now*, this minute?"

(50) This love*sick* individual sees you both as fused forever, and nothing you can say will change matters. Know that you will make major lifestyle changes in response to being pursued. Due to the unwanted *continuous* intrusion by the stalker, expect intermittent disruptions in your life. Don't let them throw you.

(51) Stalking is an on-again, off-again, ebb and flow, waxing and waning experience. Have you noticed a tapering off of incidents? A period of relative silence, or a dry spell, may lull you into feeling that it's all over, that your stalker has abandoned the pursuit, and you are finally safe. Don't be surprised when your stalker pops up again, suddenly resurfacing into a whole new series of harassment. Cycles can go on for years, escalating the violence over time.

(52) Has someone else contacted you on behalf of your stalker? It is best not to interact with *any* of his/her relatives. Often, they too, will continue their efforts, long after you've told them to stop. They have an investment in keeping their family members happy and together, so if that means keeping you two in a relationship, so be it. Do not let them sway you.

(53) Have your own family members or friends reported unexpectedly friendly overtures from your stalker? Sometimes even *they* can be persuaded to help. Inform your relatives, friends, and neighbors, in no uncertain terms, that they are never to divulge any information about you.

(54) Are you missing any items from your home, car, or work site? Or have you found odd items that had no business being there? Do some items appear to be rearranged or moved entirely?

(55) Does this person take responsibility for *any* of his/her actions? Or is justification used for all manner of unbecoming conduct? Is it clear that he/she doesn't think such behavior warrants any consequences?

(56) Schizophrenics cannot be reasoned with, or talked out of their beliefs. For instance, in his delusional state, my stalker believed himself to be a hit-man for the mafia, while my colleague's ex-husband believed himself to be Jesus Christ—a not uncommon delusion—and that he could fly. (To get a picture of this in your mind's eye, you need to know that this huge guy was a lineman for an Ivy League football team. He was always trying to jump out of hotel windows, to prove his point.) Has this person displayed any unusual thinking or odd behavior?

(57) Erotomania is a disorder of attachment. A stalker with erotomanic delusions will project all kinds of false attributes onto the victim: that the target loves him/her in return; that the target truly desires a closer relationship; that the target actually wants the two of them to always be together, but is under another's influence; that the target wants to help the stalker in some way; that the target's family and friends are in collusion in order to keep the two lovebirds apart; and so on. This is an *unchanging* belief, no matter how much the victim—or anyone else—may deny it.

(58) Ways that stalking can be stopped: forced separations via prison and/or hospital, a victim's successful move, or if the stalker focuses on another subject. Research shows that while most stalkers focus on only one person at a time, they do have sequential "love" objects. They can, and will, transfer their fixation, moving from one target to another, if somehow thwarted in their efforts.

(59) Stalking involves a series of varied activities that may often seem unimportant and unconnected when considered independently.

(57) With his delusions firmly cemented in place, my stalker conned his family into believing that—because I am an author—I was going to show him how to write a book about his *prison* experiences, and then help him to get it published. (Does this make sense to you, when I helped *put* him there?). This reasoning apparently provided enough believability for him to bring along his nephews and prowl around under my windows at night. Years later, he said that he wrote "our" story, about "our 42 years together."

(58) How discouraging to think that the only way out of repeated, intrusive, and unrelenting stalking experiences is for someone *else* to inherit the problem. Know that you don't have to move to stop the unwanted attention. Build a zone of protection and security around yourself, making it extremely difficult for anyone to monitor your whereabouts. When you become inaccessible, your stalker will look for an easier and more vulnerable victim. Know, however, that even if your stalker transfers his/her fixation to another target, there is always the option of returning to you. So keep your defenses in place.

(59) See the behavior as a whole, instead of as isolated events. Identify the pattern.

PART II

SAFETY AND HEALTH CHECKLISTS

PERSONAL SAFETY

_____ •Understand that you can't consider yourself to be completely self-reliant if you don't know how to protect yourself. Commit to improving your personal safety as a way of life. Although access to you by a stalker, abuser, or intruder can never be completely thwarted, by making smart choices—broadening your awareness, anticipating potential problems, and preparing in advance—you will vastly improve the odds of resisting an attack, or avoiding one altogether.

_____ •Get rid of that "It can't happen to me" mindset. Understand that 17,000 people are victims of violent crime _each day_ in the USA. Know that 83 out of every 100 people will be a victim of violent crime at some time in their lives. Don't bank on being one of the 17 out of 100 that remain untouched. Those are not good odds.

_____ •And it that weren't enough, know that _everyone_ is a potential target for a stalker. According to a U.S. Department of Justice study, you have a one in ten chance of being stalked (and, since it is estimated that 50 percent of all stalking victims _never_ report their contacts, you have an even higher chance of being targeted than the research suggests). No one is immune.

_____ •Project the appearance of self-assurance. Walk with confidence, purpose, and awareness. Muggers, rapists, and purse snatchers can read a person's body language to target a victim. Keep your head up, your shoulders back, and your eyes scanning the area. Using your body language, send the message that you are not a pushover, not an easy mark; that you can take care of yourself.

_____ •Look a suspicious stranger in the face. Convey the silent message that you will remember him/her, and that you're not a tentative, frightened, lost, "poor little me" victim-in-waiting.

_____ •Keep a low profile. Don't broadcast your plans or schedule.

_____ •When out and about, refrain from calling undue attention to yourself. Avoid wearing expensive outfits and flashy jewelry, which attracts muggers, purse snatchers, andpickpockets. Dress casually.

_____ •Do not wear restrictive clothing, high heels, or flip-flops when out shopping. Be relaxed and comfortable. Wear shoes in which you can easily run, if need be.

_____ •Understand that neck scarves and long necklaces can be used for choke holds, while pony tails make it easy to grab you from behind, jerking your head back. Be prepared to fight back.

_____ •When in line (whether at banks, markets, or stores), check to see if anyone seems unduly interested in watching the transactions.

_____ •Do not flash your money. Be discreet and stash your cash quickly.

_____ •Never leave your purse in a shopping cart. It's too easy to be distracted, even when you're standing right next to it. (One Christmas, while shopping in a toy mart, my wallet was lifted from my purse in the cart. I knew what the two men looked like, and could identify them, but the manager wouldn't help. I became more upset about *his* reaction than the fact that my money and charge cards were gone forever. He refused to use the loudspeaker to warn holiday shoppers that there were thieves in the crowd, as it might dampen their spirits.)

_____ •Know where you are at all times. If in an unfamiliar place, check the information kiosk or map directories for the general layout of the area. Specifically check for security or police posts, community safety centers, emergency exits, and public phones.

_____ •Ignore drunks whenever possible. Quickly move away, as they may be muggers, purse snatchers, or pickpockets in disguise.

_____ •Experts maintain that you keep a distance of two arm-lengths from a stranger. Of course, that's hard to do if you're in a popular public place with a crush of people, but keep this in mind when in a less crowded area.

_____ •If accosted by several petty hoodlums, ignore their taunts. Never show fear or anger. Always keep in mind that a battered ego is better than a battered body.

_____ •If someone points a gun at you demanding money, give up your cash! Your life is worth more than your wallet, watch, or credit cards.

_____ •Never pursue an attacker. True, it goes against the grain, but remember: Safety first! (I once chased a guy that had just bashed in the windshields of twelve cars with a baseball bat—and was gaining on him, in my heels, yet—before a car careened down the street, and he dove into it. To this day, I don't know what I would have done had I actually *caught* him, since he was much taller and stronger than I. My body would probably have been suffering a number of needless aches and pains.) Don't get carried away.

_____ •Make concrete plans for how to get away from a stalker, abuser, or intruder, at home, work, school, or out in public.

_____ •Acquaint yourself with fastest route to the police or sheriff's departments, the fire department, or campus security.

_____ •Know the closest 24-hour stores, fitness centers, restaurants, and other areas where people will be at all times.

_____ •Locate the nearest pay phones before you may need them. Carry change, even if you have a cell phone.

_____ •Know the location of several motels—in which the parking can't be seen from the street—in case it is ever unwise to go home.

_____ •Familiarize yourself with local shelters. They are open for women and children from all incomes and ethnic groups. (Communities also need to support men who are being abused, but, at this time, I know of only one such shelter in Los Angeles: The Antelope Valley Domestic Violence Council/Valley Oasis Shelter in Lancaster. Logistically, shelters can't provide for both women and men at the same facility, because of the shared living space and communal facilities.) These come-as-you-are havens, represent the modern-day equivalent of the

Underground Railroad. Shelters offer protection, while, at the same time, dispensing education, guidance, support, and understanding.

_____ •Be prepared to fight back—physically, mentally and emotionally—*before* the need arises. Be confident of your ability to defend yourself under any and all unforeseen situations. Maintain your boundaries. Refuse to be a pulp-fiction victim.

_____ •Understand that your reaction to an attack should depend upon how the circumstance unfolds. This is not a one-size-fits-all experience, no matter what you hear or read. You must keep assessing the attacker and the environment, while searching for suitable options. Only *you* can determine whether to stall for time, scream for help, fight back, run, or if completely overpowered, yield. Your response will differ according to each situation.

_____ •Whatever happens, be a good witness. Observe and remember as much as you can. Your mission is to keep calm. (One nine-year-old who was kidnapped remembered the address number of the house to which she had been taken, along with the fact that they had a pizza delivery. The police put those two facts together, and immediately arrested the abductor.)

_____ •If verbally assaulted, respond in kind. Instead of being a cream puff, if you demonstrate real anger, you are less likely to be assaulted. Know that neither crying nor pleading works.

_____ •If you lack a raging rhinoceros attitude, if getting in someone's face, thumping-your-chest, and foul language just isn't your cup of tea, then you must *practice*. Shut your door, turn on the tub water or shower full force, blast the radio, and yell into the mirror. You must thoroughly *believe* that you are worth defending.

_____ •Yelling "No!", "Stop!", "Get away from me!" "Back off!", or loudly swearing at your attacker may prevent further harassment. Experts tell us to attract attention in public places, by screaming, "I don't know him/her!" and "Please call the police!" Oddly, research tells us that yelling "Help!" doesn't work. (The plain and ugly truth is that people would rather not get involved. Recall the famous New York City incident, in which Kitty Genovese was chased by her assailant and attacked three different times, on the street, within a half-hour period, while 38 witnesses watched and did nothing.) Police recommend that you yell "Fire!" instead.

_____ •Once you use aggressive language, don't back down. Continue to be on the offensive and establish distance. This is no time to return to your sweet disposition, good manners, and quiet tone. Studies show that as much as 80 percent of potential assaults are prevented by assertive responses.

_____ •Although an attacker usually has the advantage in size and strength, experts say that neither are the most important components in a fight. Recognize that guts and determination are what really count in a battle. By fighting back, you have the element of surprise on your side.

_____ •There must be no hesitation in your actions. This is not the time to consider philosophical or spiritual distinctions. Determine to *survive*. Mull it over later.

_____ •Attach your keys to a mini-baton (sometimes called a Kubotan or Persuader), which is a slender stick, three and a half to five and a half inches long, with an attached key ring at one end. It can expand your personal space, and is an effective defense weapon, if you know how to use it. (It is used by law enforcement personnel.) I use a bracelet-sized key ring to whip my keys around, extending the distance between an aggressor and myself. You need to keep your assailant as far away as possible.

_____ •Umbrellas, canes, and belts can also be used to extend your boundaries, although they will be easier for an attacker to grab and use against you.

_____ •If you have no choice but to defend yourself, forget the Marquis of Queensbury rules. This is a no-holds-barred situation: FIGHT DIRTY. Do as much damage in as little time as possible. Hit, punch, and slash. Refuse to be a victim: strike down or thrust out with your heel. Stomp feet and shins. Kick the front or sides of kneecaps, the groin, the stomach, the head. Go for the face. Strike an attacker with the heel of your palm, hitting the nose. Cup your hands and box the ears. Jab at the Adam's apple or side of the neck. Gouge the eyes. Punch the temple. Lace the fingers of both your hands together in a two-handed grip and swing. Spear your elbows into ribs. Scratch to get that DNA under your fingernails! Jerk out clumps of hair, for further evidence. Grab, pull, and twist whatever. (Recall the movie "Miss Congeniality," in which Sandra Bullock says to remember the word *sing*, and aim for the solar plexus, instep, nose, and groin.) Don't give the stalker, rapist, or intruder a chance to think or recover. Keep your blows coming with full force, never giving your assailant a break. You may well be fighting for your life.

_____　•According to research, a man can knock down a female victim in a matter of six seconds (or seven, when climbing through a window!), so you also need to know how to fight from a ground position. Use not only your arms, but the strength in your hips and legs, as well. Get down on the floor and practice bicycle kicking!

_____　•Know that rape is one of the most common crimes against women.

_____　•Studies also show that women are less likely to be raped, if they resist. The extra time and effort involved—plus the added noise factor— provides more chance of discovery, so the rapist may opt for easier prey. Of course, if your attacker is under the influence of drugs or alcohol, logic will not be a factor. Loudly scream and yell. (Mental health experts contend that you will suffer far less psychological trauma if you put up a resistance.)

_____　•Explore the many facets of self-defense. Read books by self-defense experts (see Recommended Reading), and magazines (*Self Defense for Women*), that specifically deal with the subject. You have more options than you may realize.

_____　•Take a self-defense course, such as Impact, Rape Aggression Defense (RAD) and the American Women's Defense Association, or classes hosted by local women's groups or city recreation. Build self-reliance and confidence in your ability to defend yourself. You will learn contact fighting, and can take part in mock assaults (by a mock assailant, who wears protective padded gear, so you can fight back with full force). You'll also learn how to block, punch, and get out of choke holds. Continue to practice, to make sure these defensive moves are in your muscle memory, so your responses will be automatic. (I was a national TV guest on 'The Gordon Elliot Show," speaking about my stalking experiences. Unbeknownst to me, I had been singled out for a mock attack by a Model Mugging trainer. I knocked the guy down and stomped him, as the crowd cheered. I was most surprised, but pleased, with my immediate reaction.) No matter what your height or weight, fitness level, or personal handicap, know that such contact fighting courses are designed with you in mind. The strikes, holds, locks, and throws that are taught work for anyone. Watch several different classes, before choosing one that feels right. (Look for boundary setting and ferocity development, as well as defensive techniques.) Better yet, take several. You might want to start out with a class that is a few hours long, then a full day class, and work up to a 20-hour course. If you feel nervous about signing up for such a class, take a friend along for mutual support.

_____ •If no self defense, contact fighting, or martial arts courses are available in your area, get some good self-defense videos and learn from them. If unavailable in your library, try Melissa Soalt's excellent video series *Fierce and Female* (www.dr-ruthless.com/frameset.htm).

_____ •If your money is earmarked for other security measures, practice doing some damage on a pillow. Visualize an attacker's head, feet, or stomach. Put some energy and power behind those kicks and punches.

_____ •Read about personal non-lethal weapons. Familiarize yourself with what is available (mini-batons, pepper spray, and stun guns, as well as improvised weapons). Examine all your options, as there are pros and cons to each. Understand that simply *buying* or *carrying* non-lethal weapons, should not give you a false confidence of protection. Commit to learning how to use them effectively.

_____ •Check the pepper spray laws in your area. In some states it is illegal to use, while others require that you take a class, or watch a specific video, before being allowed to carry it.

_____ •Pepper spray is considered to be one of the best non-lethal self-defense tools you can use. Pepper spray—oleoresin capsicum or OC—is both safe and effective, in the 5 to 10 percent range. (It has replaced the use of tear gas and mace.) Do not buy OC that is mixed with anything else, and check the expiration date. The two-ounce canister is best for your purposes (the container bottom is about the size of a quarter). Experts caution that you carry it in your strong hand, in the ready-to-use position, or to keep your hand on it while in your purse or pocket, whenever you are uneasy, or walking to and from your house or car. (Police, FBI, and mail carriers, have used this spray effectively, for decades.) Pepper spray works best at a 4 to 6 foot range. Spray several short bursts directly onto the face of your assailant, hold your breath, and run. Immediately call and report the incident to the police.

_____ •Know that pepper spray is best used *before* a crime is about to take place, such as a carjacking, mugging, or rape. Although fast-acting, it is not instantaneous, and if a gun, knife, or bat attack is already in progress—and it will take only a few seconds to complete the assault—pepper spray is less likely to be effective. Also, know that it doesn't necessarily have the same effect on everyone.

_____ •The downside of pepper spray is that you can't use it in a small, closed space—such as a car, an elevator, or tiny room—without spraying yourself in the process. If you spray in a larger office or room, get out quickly and shut the door, to keep the spray contained in that area alone. (My husband and I were eating dinner at a restaurant in Lakewood, and watched as a dozen police cars, and every ambulance in the city and nearby areas, converged in the parking lot across the street. We thought a gang shooting had just taken place. Not so. Pepper spray had been "accidentally" dropped in a movie theater, and the entire complex had to be evacuated, as the spray spread into the ventilation system, polluting all of the rooms. The same thing happened in a couple of local schools. Pepper spray is powerful, but not lethal.) Consider getting a foam or a stream nozzle, instead of the cone-shaped spray or foggers nozzle, to limit the area of contamination.

_____ •If you do manage to get the spray on yourself, don't rub your eyes. Use cool water. Sit in front of a fan for fresh air. Within 45 minutes to an hour, you should be back to normal. If not, get medical attention.

_____ •Keep your pepper spray out of the reach of children.

_____ •Be careful of how you dispose of the pepper spray canisters.

_____ •Stun guns are not legal in all states. Check it out first, before purchasing one.

_____ •Stun guns are more useful as a deterrant, than as an actual weapon. They are only usable when firmly placed against the skin of your attacker, and held for up to four seconds, and who is going to allow you to do that? Furthermore, when in that close proximity, a stun gun would be easy to take away and use against yourself. Although sold in a variety of sizes and voltages—from 25,000 to 100,000—it doesn't allow you a distance defense. (Pilots are now using stun guns in cockpits.)

_____ •You need to be psychologically ready to deal with guns, and come to terms with them. Could you shoot someone who was going to kidnap your child? Could you shoot someone who was going to hurt a loved one? Could you shoot someone who was attacking you?

_____ •If you are as gunshy as I was, take the opportunity to overcome your reluctance to have anything to do with firearms. Harness your alarm, and relieve some of your anxiety, by becoming familiar with handguns: browse through various gun stores and gun shows, just to get a feel for them, and be comfortable around them. (Wanting to face my fear, the first time I walked into a gun store alone, I was scared to death. It was such an alien atmosphere; I raced up and down the aisles at a mad clip. I persevered, however, and several visits later, it became an easier environment to deal with.) Talk with salespeople, and peruse gun books and magazines (such as _Women & Guns_) on the subject. Do your homework.

_____ •If you are considering a handgun for personal protection, regardless of whether you feel you can handle it physically or emotionally, get some training. Sign up to take a gun course. (This was extremely difficult for me to begin, having always been opposed to violence as a way of settling disputes. But I finally came to realize the tremendous moral difference between criminal assault and self-defense.) Know that you can take firearms training _without_ the commitment of buying a gun. If a school or instructor says they don't lend guns, look for another. (As one expert put it: You wouldn't buy a horse just to take riding lessons, would you?) You will be absolutely amazed at what you learn, and you will be better prepared afterwards to assess whether you should become a gun owner.

_____ •Educate yourself concerning your city, state, and federal gun licensing and other gun-related laws. Check out possible legal problems that might ensue from owning or discharging a gun. Be responsible.

_____ •Before opting for owning a gun, you must rid yourself of the fear, anxiety, and mystique surrounding having one in the house. Granted, if guns are used irresponsibly, they can be deadly, but so can fire, cars, booze, and knives. Change your mindset: consider a handgun to be a necessary household safety tool, like a smoke alarm or fire extinguisher; or simply view it as a useful machine, to use as needed, like an iron, toaster, or vacuum cleaner. Realize that the power of a gun *equalizes* your situation with that of the overpowering size, strength, and brute force of a stalker or rapist.

_____ •If you decide that a gun is an effective deterrent, you may consider buying one. Know at the outset, however, that owning a handgun involves investing not only money, but a considerable amount of time, effort, and energy. Make a responsible decision.

_____ •Take your time choosing the model and weight that is appropriate for your hand size and strength. It must not only feel comfortable in your hand, and be light enough to easily handle, but powerful enough to be effective. Do your research, and find a handgun within your price range. (Know upfront, that it is much easier for a beginner to load and fire revolvers than semi-automatic pistols.)

_____ •Along with your handgun and ammunition, you must also buy a pistol cleaning kit. You need to clean your weapon after every practice session.

_____ •Take safety precautions, especially if you have youngsters living in your house. Guns that aren't used for defense should be locked up, with the ammunition locked up separately. Guns that *are* used for defense need to be kept loaded, in a lockbox (which is a small safe designed to hold a loaded gun). This is the best way to keep your defense gun ready for emergencies, but inaccessible to children, immature teens, or others. (Lockboxes come with a wide variety of locking mechanisms, from pushbuttons to electric locks, in all price ranges. A perfectly adequate lockbox sells for well under a hundred dollars.)

_____ •Don't let the simple fact that you own a handgun lull you into a false sense of safety. After your initial training, you need to practice loading and unloading your gun twice a day, and practice target shooting at a range at least once a month. Know upfront that it can be mentally demanding and physically exhausting. Make sure your reactions remain in your muscle memory by continuing to practice. Make it a habit.

_____ •Practice quickly loading and unloading your weapon in the dark. This, too, needs to be a part of your muscle memory.

_____ •Understand that becoming skillful in firing at a bull's eye or stationary paper silhouette is quite different than firing at a moving human being. Not to mention, the stress factor involved. There is a vast difference between what is termed "practical shooting" (reloading, marksmanship, and tactics) and that of "combat shooting" (self-defense situations and shooting under pressure). Check to see if action training is offered locally.

_____ •After taking a gun course, and having had sufficient practice at training sessions, you may feel the need to apply for a concealed weapon license. The application may be expensive, and, depending where you live, there is no guarantee that you will be able to obtain one. Licenses are difficult—if not impossible—to get in certain areas. (I had to threaten my local police department with a lawsuit, before finally obtaining one, becoming the first private citizen in the city to be issued such a license.) However, other areas actually promote the idea, such as Louisiana Governor Mike Foster, who counsels women on self-protection, "You have the right to get a gun permit."

_____ •Check your state laws concerning concealed weapons, as some states make it illegal to carry one. And, depending on the city, there are limits as to where you can carry a concealed weapon even *with* a license.

_____ •If you are able to obtain a concealed weapon license, you may want to consider how best to carry your weapon in public. (One woman has carried her gun around in a shoebox, for years.) More women carry guns in their purses than anywhere else. As such, it is far better to buy a special holster purse than to carry your gun around in a regular purse (it won't be flashed accidentally while digging around for loose change or lipstick; it will always be in the same place, not upside-down, with your wallet on it; it won't get tangled up with other stuff in the bottom of your purse; and, it has easy access). If a purse holster doesn't appeal to you, there are a variety of holsters, in leather, plastic, or mesh: an ankle holster, or one designed to be worn in the small of your back, or a holster that rides on your hip, as well as a shoulder rig. Whatever you buy, wear it around the house, to get used to the extra weight, before you go out in public. It may make you feel slightly uncomfortable and off balance, at first. Loose jackets can cover up the bulge it makes. If you wear form-fitting clothes, this may present a problem.

_____ •Keep a list of emergency numbers in your wallet, pocket, or purse. In times of crisis, it is easy to forget numbers entirely or transpose them, no matter how perfect your memory usually performs. Don't depend upon your memory in a time of stress. Understand that the sudden strain of a situation can change your normal reactions. (I used to have a mind like a steel trap; now it's Swiss cheese.)

_____ •Keep a log of every time your stalker tries to contact you: jot down the date, time, and the nature of the contact. Include the names and phone numbers of anywitnesses. Report them to the police.

_____ •Keep track of all unidentified hang-up calls, disguised calls, obscene calls, and odd e-mail messages.

_____ •Change your e-mail address if you are getting unwanted messages.

_____ •Keep taped phone messages as evidence. Have a stack of new answering machine cassettes handy, so you won't accidentally record over those you need to keep.

_____ •Keep a list of magazines, goods, and materials sent to you that you didn't order. Some stalkers will sign you up for tons of varied and unwanted items, just to jerk your chain. While going through the tedious task of returning items and canceling your charge cards, you'll be thinking of your stalker, which is like a double bonus for him/her.

_____ •Similarly, keep a list of anything that has has been canceled in your name (telephone, utilities, charge accounts, newspapers, memberships, and rerouted mail. Someone cancelled my Business ATM card. How can *that* happen?)

_____ •Keep all letters, cards, notes, e-mails, faxes, and mailed photographs in your file. If any letters or pictures are written or smeared with blood, encase them in plastic after they've dried, for fingerprint evidence. Touch only the edges. Keep everything that is even mildly suspicious. What you think is important may differ from what the police deem important. (I was looking at my stalker's letters from a psychological point of view, whereas the police were looking for specifics that the law covers).

_____ •Even when grossed out, keep all unwanted gifts (vials of blood, urine, feces, and the like) for DNA evidence. The police will take charge of these items.

_____ •Use a camera or video recorder to photograph perishable items (dead flowers, cockroaches, rats, or animal carcasses, et ceterra), spray-painted words and/or pictures (on walls, fences, garages, or sidewalks), and vandalism (car, house, or property). Experts suggest documenting photos by including a dated newspaper in the picture or using film that is automatically dated. Since implied messages are now considered to be threatening behavior in courts, victims are taking photos of their driveways—upon which roofing tacks, nails, and broken glass were scattered; their lawns—in which chemicals have deadened the grass or flowers; as well as their spray-painted vehicles. I recently saw a car parked in front of a local high school with the word "Puta" scrawled all over it, about a hundred times, in varying sizes. Nice.

_____ •Do not acknowledge that you've received anything. Never answer letters. Never return anything!

_____ •Make three or four photo copies each. Keep one set for your personal files in your safety deposit box. Give one set to the police. Keep a set for convenient show-and-tell purposes, with family, friends, and other interested parties, at your residence. On occasion, the media will ask to use a set. (A word to the wise: It has been my experience that loaned photos are either not returned at all, or not returned in a timely fashion, or not returned in pristine shape.)

_____ •Determine to live a more cautious life. Avoid areas that your stalker is known to frequent. Use your common sense. Don't needlessly place yourself in harms way. Safety is the issue, not fairness (which took me far too long to come to terms with).

_____ •Find ways to make yourself difficult to track. Don't make yourself a target. (I reluctantly gave up my nightly walks through the park. Again, it's not fair, but it's a safety issue. It's easier to prevent crimes than to solve them. Remember the Central Park Jogger, Trisha Meili, who was beaten, raped, and left for dead, on April 19, 1987, who miraculously came out of a comma five and a half weeks later.) The old adage is true: It's better to be safe than sorry.

_____ •Vary your routine. If a tracker knows your schedule, you are at risk anytime, any place, anywhere. (I was determined not to do things differently, but finally came to the realization that by not making any changes, I would actually be *helping* my stalker. My own habits were seemingly set in cement, when he phoned me at the hair salon one Saturday morning, from prison. That wake-up call caused me to make immediate changes thereafter). Intermittently vary the places you shop and use for recreation. Don't be predictable.

_____ •Obtain a TRO (Temporary Restraining Order)—which is in effect for a period of 14 days in California. Getting a TRO is the hoop you have to jump through to prove to the courts that you are committed to the process, before you can return for an extension. It's a royal pain, but *do it anyway.* (Understand that restraining orders are issued at the rate of more than one thousand a day in the USA, so you are not alone.) Keep your mind off the inconvenience, and on your long-term goal: survival.

_____ •Pay a Marshall (at the same courthouse) or a private investigator to hand-deliver the TRO. You don't want to deal with it in any way whatsoever. You want the restraining order in force, as soon as possible. In any case, you don't want to place yourself or a family member in jeopardy.

_____ •Petition to have the stalker pay for this service *only* if it presents a financial hardship for you, and doesn't prolong your court schedule.

_____ •Go back to court and obtain the restraining order. The process is exhausting, but necessary. Keep in mind that if you are going through a stalking experience, you can handle this inconvenience, also.

_____ •Request a permanent protective order.

_____ •Once the TRO is received, notify your police department that you have a protective order. (I notified the three police agencies involved in my case: the city in which I lived, the city in which my stalker lived, and the city in which I worked).

_____ •Understand at the outset that the restraining order—that flimsy little piece of paper—will not actually *restrain* your stalker, nor will it *protect* you physically. It will not *save* you from bullets, knives, blunt objects, or whatever else may be aimed at you. (I once had vinegar spewed on me from a spray bottle, while I was standing in line at the movies. Thank God it wasn't something else!) It just makes everything official, and gives any upcoming complaints credibility. If you can say that you have a current restraining order in effect, those are like the *magic words* to receive instant action. (When my stalker was chased, caught, and detained, before the police could even check him out, the first question I was asked, was, "Do you have a restraining order currently in effect?" When I said yes, the officer called downtown to verify that fact, and then she went back, searched his car, found a gun and ample ammunition, and arrested him.) Stalking behavior is no longer treated as merely an "infatuation," a case of overzealous "puppy love," or simply a "family matter," ignored by the police and the courts. It is now considered to be an act of trespassing, breaking and entering, vandalism, robbery, rape, or kidnapping, which are all criminal matters, and can no longer be overlooked by the law.

_____ •Make numerous copies of your restraining order.

_____ •Keep the original restraining order in your safety deposit box. Make a separate file for these papers, as they will increase, due to various stalking experiences.

_____ •There is a difference of opinion concerning the resultant stalker behavior after a retraining order has been received by the stalker. Some experts expect the violence to escalate immediately. Others expect the stalking behavior to lessen in the short-term, directly after a restraining order has been served, but fully expect it to escalate later. Research shows that after about a six-month period, the long-term behavior is unaffected. Prepare for either possibility.

_____ •The next time the line is crossed—and, trust me, it more than likely *will*, since 80 percent of all restraining orders are violated—and your stalker is once again found on your block, or follows you, or harasses you in any way, he/she will be arrested, charged, and held accountable. (My stalker wrote me a letter, while out on early parole, and was immediately returned to prison to complete his original sentence.)

_____ •Request copies of all police reports for your own files. (I didn't know that was even a possibility.)

_____ •Record the names and badge numbers of all officers involved.

_____ •Request the PD pamphlets that explain your rights.

_____ •File such important papers right away, as they can easily get lost in the shuffle. (In the business world, I am known for being organized and efficient, able to place my hands on any item within minutes. But I was always so rattled after I saw the police, that I had papers stashed everywhere, and consequently, couldn't find them when I needed them.) Designate *one* place—a drawer or a box—to pile such important reports, until you can function normally, and deal with them intelligently. Then sort and file your papers carefully for easy reference.

_____ •Have duplicate car and house keys made. Keep them in a secure place.

_____ •When dealing with a stalker or an abuser, keep an overnight bag in the trunk of your car, or at a friend's house, or a locker at the airport, bus or train station, or even at your 24-hour health club. Pack it with a few clothes, incidentals, money, duplicate keys, glasses or contact lenses, and medications. Also include ID, a copy of your restraining order and stalking log, a list of emergency numbers, and other important papers, in case you must relocate quickly. Hopefully, you'll never need to use it, but it'll give you a feeling of security, nonetheless.

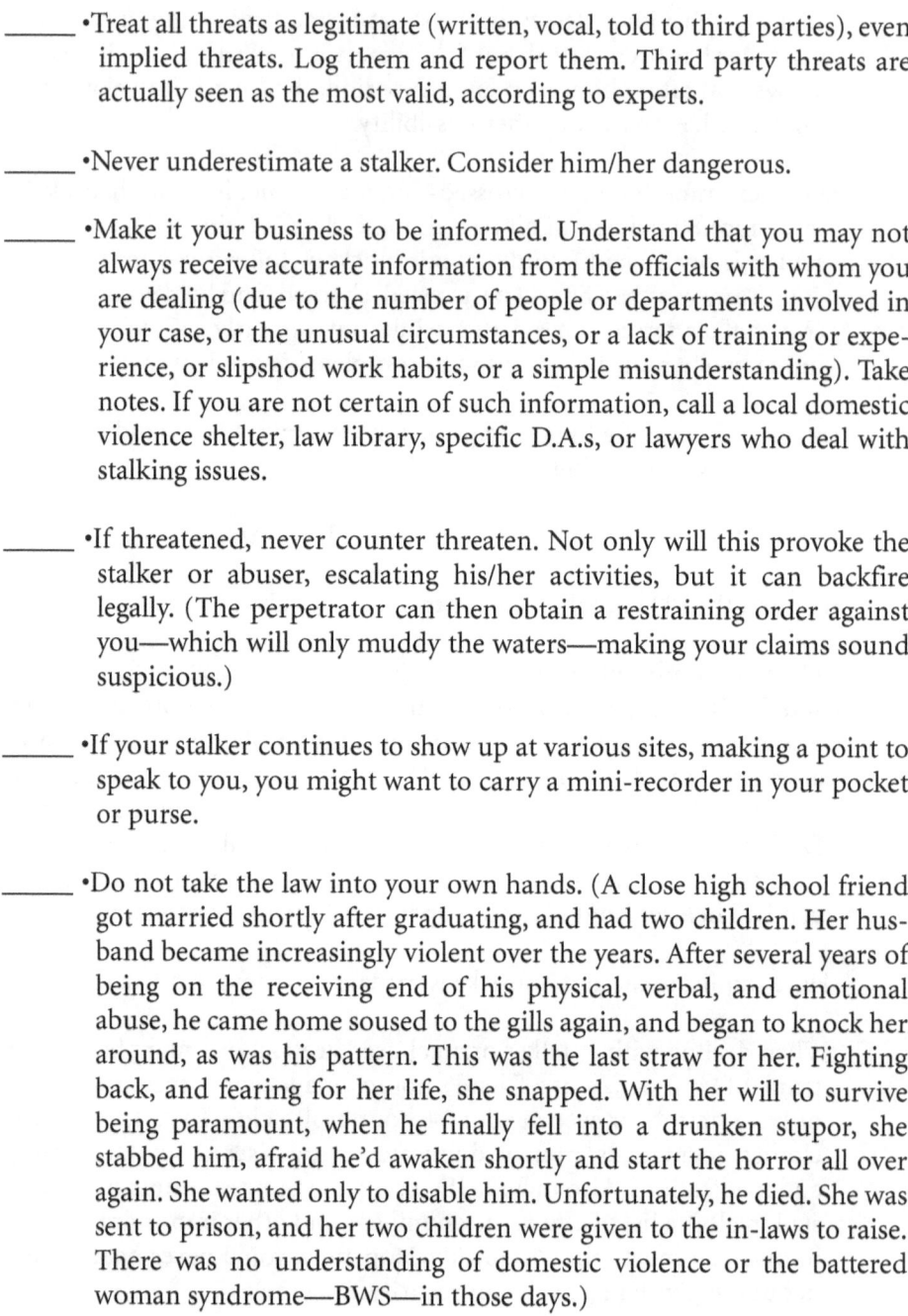

_____ •Treat all threats as legitimate (written, vocal, told to third parties), even implied threats. Log them and report them. Third party threats are actually seen as the most valid, according to experts.

_____ •Never underestimate a stalker. Consider him/her dangerous.

_____ •Make it your business to be informed. Understand that you may not always receive accurate information from the officials with whom you are dealing (due to the number of people or departments involved in your case, or the unusual circumstances, or a lack of training or experience, or slipshod work habits, or a simple misunderstanding). Take notes. If you are not certain of such information, call a local domestic violence shelter, law library, specific D.A.s, or lawyers who deal with stalking issues.

_____ •If threatened, never counter threaten. Not only will this provoke the stalker or abuser, escalating his/her activities, but it can backfire legally. (The perpetrator can then obtain a restraining order against you—which will only muddy the waters—making your claims sound suspicious.)

_____ •If your stalker continues to show up at various sites, making a point to speak to you, you might want to carry a mini-recorder in your pocket or purse.

_____ •Do not take the law into your own hands. (A close high school friend got married shortly after graduating, and had two children. Her husband became increasingly violent over the years. After several years of being on the receiving end of his physical, verbal, and emotional abuse, he came home soused to the gills again, and began to knock her around, as was his pattern. This was the last straw for her. Fighting back, and fearing for her life, she snapped. With her will to survive being paramount, when he finally fell into a drunken stupor, she stabbed him, afraid he'd awaken shortly and start the horror all over again. She wanted only to disable him. Unfortunately, he died. She was sent to prison, and her two children were given to the in-laws to raise. There was no understanding of domestic violence or the battered woman syndrome—BWS—in those days.)

_____ •If you feel that you are not receiving proper police support, know that you have the right to go directly to the District Attorney, to have your case reviewed. (I wish I had known this much earlier. Still, even with the laws on the books, it has taken incidents like the following, for stalking victims to be taken seriously: In 1996, six years after the original stalking law went into affect, a San Francisco woman appealed to sheriff's deputies to enforce her restraining order, to no avail. Repeatedly harassed, threatened, and stalked, she pleaded for help, and was ignored by officers on at least nine different occasions. After she was murdered, her family sued. In 2002, the settlement reached required Sonoma County to pay one million dollars to the woman's mother and her three children, for the department's inaction. Sheriff's deputies and police officers are now acutely aware of the possible results of inattention to stalking matters.)

HOME SAFETY

_____ •Commit to improving your home safety. Think of this as a do-it-yourself project. Understand that while there is no such thing as a totally secure residence, you can certainly take steps to improve your safety measures to keep intruders out. Check for the weakest link in your home defense.

_____ •Repair doors as soon as you notice that they stick, are warped, or in need of new hardware.

_____ •Install metal or heavy solid wood doors that a foot cannot kick through.

_____ •Do not buy a fancy front door with inset stained glass windows. You don't want anyone peering inside the foyer or living room, without your knowledge. And although beautiful, the slender, decorative, full-length side panel windows—often placed on either side of a front door—represent a security risk. Board them up.

_____ •Experts suggest that you use a fisheye peephole—wide angle, one way viewers—on your outside doors. (I purposely did *not* have one installed in my new door, as I can easily look out the wooden slats of a side wall window.) Still, if you have no other way to see your visitors, you may need to install one.

_____ •If you have no peephole, use chains on the outside doors, to see who is knocking. Understand that chains will only slow down intruders, but will never stop them completely, as they can be easily snapped, or severed with bolt cutters. However, they may afford you the few seconds needed, to get to safety.

_____ •Install heavy-duty, top-of-the-line deadbolts—that protrude at least two inches—on all exterior doors. They are far superior to chains. This is money well spent. You may opt for secondary locks, as well.

_____ •Install steel screen doors with security locks and hinges.

_____ •Experts tell us that windows positioned within a 40-inch reach of door locks are a security risk. Consider the placement of your windows.

_____ •Always account for every single house door and garage key. If missing one, have your locks changed. Remember: Safety before convenience.

_____ •Do not leave a spare key in a planter, under the welcome mat, on top of the doorframe, or anywhere outside. And, unless you have a truckload of rocks around your house, don't use one of those rock hide-a-keys, since you'd be gambling that an intruder doesn't know about them. Sure it's a pain, but this is a matter of security. Give a key to trusted neighbors. (The best fifty dollars I ever spent was when I locked myself out of the house, and had to call a locksmith. What a great feeling of safety!)

_____ •Consider installing a security camera at the front door.

_____ •Try giving a retired stay-at-home neighbor a video camera, to record evidence of suspicious behavior (trespassing, forced entry, robbery, vandalizing, mail tampering, and the like).

_____ •A videotape shot from a neighbor's surveillance camera clearly shows how an intruder targeted a nine-year-old girl. The man brutally beat the mother and the son, and abducted the young girl. From the tape, investigators knew what the man looked like, as well as the make, model, and color of his car. An Amber alert was issued, and the man was caught the next day. You might consider using one.

_____ •Place a permanent NO SOLICITORS or NO PEDDLERS or a DO NOT DISTURB or DAY SLEEPER sign by the front door.

_____ •Place a permanent NO TRESPASSING or NO LOITERING sign on your property. Discourage strangers coming to your house.

_____ •If you are a woman living by yourself, and a phone solicitor or door-to-door salesperson asks to speak to "the man of the house," say that he's working in the back yard, or is busy, or napping, and cannot be disturbed. Never let a stranger know that you live alone, or are alone at that moment. Your living arrangements are no one's business.

_____ •Never open your door before identifying strangers. Ask to see proper identification of all repair and delivery people.

_____ •If a stranger asks to use your phone, no matter what dire emergency he/she may plead, call the police for them. Don't open the door. Many home invasions are initiated in this manner.

_____ •If you have ordered an item to be delivered (food, flowers, medicine, a small package, and the like), but don't know the delivery people on sight, consider meeting them outside on your porch, or in the lobby of your building—where others can be watching. Do not give intruders access to your open door in which to quickly gain entrance. After all, if they're driving their own cars, you don't know if this is the real delivery person, or a Home Invader. Consider the pros and cons of pick-up over delivery. Do not place your name on delivery orders.

_____ •Refuse to open the door at night for any reason. Make this a personal rule! Let your neighbors and friends know. They will certainly understand, although I've actually had young door-to-door salespeople argue with me—shouting through my closed door—about my policy. Can you *believe*? Don't bother explaining. Just don't answer the door.

_____ •Yes, a big dog can provide another alarm system, but if you're not a dog lover, or you work odd hours, have limited space, or are gone much of the time, this is definitely not the right choice for you. If you decide to obtain a dog for security, you must consider the specific breed, as well as the individual characteristics of the dog. Understand that a warm, trusting, playful pet will happily make friends with strangers, providing you with a false sense of security. Plus, if you have to continually open the door to let it in and out, or walk the dog at night, you are defeating the purpose. Is there a barking ordinance in effect in your area? A Leash law? You must also consider whether an aggressive dog will present a risk to visitors and neighborhood children. Do you carry the proper insurance? Post a BEWARE OF DOG sign, in any case.

_____ •If you have a doggie door installed in your back door, make sure that it is a small opening, and that a long arm (or a small child) cannot slide through and reach the doorknob.

_____ •If you have a kitchen/back door with a large window in it, replace it with a solid door. The window can easily be broken, allowing an intruder to use the inside doorknob to easily open the door.

_____ •Consider installing shatterproof glass in your windows, French doors, and skylights.

_____ •Know that French doors and louvered windowpanes are easy to force open. Consider replacing them.

_____ •Install sliding-bolt locks at both the top and bottom of all French doors.

_____ •Ensure that all your windows have sturdy locks, including the garage window. And keep them locked.

_____ •Keep doors and windows locked, even when you're on the property (patio, garden, pool, or garage). Don't give an intruder the opportunity to slip in your house unnoticed. (One out of four burglars and most rapists enter a house through unlocked windows or doors.)

_____ •Make it a nightly ritual to re-check both doors and windows, to make sure that they are locked.

_____ •Use a dowel, or insert eye bolts, or even just a nail, in all sliding windows, to keep them from being fully opened.

_____ •Use a special steel bar or wooden bar, for your sliding doors, to keep them from being opened. (I have used a sawed-off broom handle for years!)

_____ •Consider investing in bars that lock across the center of sliding glass windows.

_____ •Always keep your drapes/shades/shutters closed at night. Draw them *before* switching on the lights, or you'll be backlit. You do not want to encourage voyeurs, nor provide an easy target for a stalker or rapist. (When I was in my late twenties, I had fallen asleep one night, while viewing a spectacular moon. I awoke in the morning to see a face staring at me through my bedroom window. When I yelped in surprise— hastily pulling the sheets over me—the man beat a hasty retreat down the backside of my apartment building, never to be seen again. Boy, did I learn my lesson!)

_____ •Replace sheer, gauzy curtains. Make sure your drapes are heavy, to lesson an intruder's ability to track your movements by your silhouette, or simply by watching the lights being flicked off from room to room.

_____ •Consider putting several locks on your bedroom door, if it will make you feel more safe and secure. Install them with longer screws.

_____ •Never ever sleep with your bedroom windows open. (One night, a friend was in deep sleep, when a foot landed solidly on his face, as a burglar was climbing through the window directly over his bed. By the time he got his wits about him, and reacted, the burglar was long gone.) Use an air-conditioner.

_____ •Make sure your air-conditioner is solidly bolted into the window frame, so it can't be either pulled out or pushed in, allowing an intruder easy access.

_____ •If concerned that you won't hear break-ins at night, place Baby Monitors in the rooms furthest from your bedroom. Or, instead, you can hang large windchimes, bells, or anything that will make noise if jostled, across the windows.

_____ •Turn off the Baby Monitors when not in use, as others can eavesdrop on your private conversations, in the same way that those on cordless phones and hearing aides can be picked up by scanners.

_____ •Keep a cellular phone by your bed, with an automatic 911 dial feature to use in the dark. When calling, always announce your location *first*, then add details, as time permits.

_____ •Victims are often so fearful that they sleep with a gun, a knife, or some kind of spray under their pillows, which is not only lumpy, but extremely unsafe. (Keep the lockbox by your bed: if you're awake enough to get through the lock in the box, then you're alert enough to use the gun safely, and won't be shooting your foot or your cat. Consider using Bed Pockets or Bed Caddies—that fit between the mattress and bedsprings, that hang alongside your bed—to house any other weapons you require). Many also sleep with a baseball bat under their beds.

_____ •If you live in a cold climate, keep coats, hats, and gloves close to your outside doors for easy access in an emergency.

_____ •Remove all large bushes or hedges (or at least cut them down below the window ledges) to eliminate possible hiding places, as well as to broaden your field of vision from inside the house.

_____ •If shrubs must stay, strategically place spotlights on them for illumination. Install ground lighting along the flowerbeds.

_____ •Flood water directly underneath your windows at night. Check for footprints or disturbed ground area, in the early morning, to see if you are being watched. Take photographs, to control your paranoia, if nothing else.

_____ •Invest in a Xeriscape garden made of cacti, thick, prickly plants, and small pebbles—to be placed under your most vulnerable windows—to deter entry therefrom. (A neighbor covered his entire front lawn with gravel. Although esthetically challenged, an intruder can never sneak upon that property without his/her crunching footsteps sounding the alarm.)

_____ •Install motion-sensitive floodlights around your property. (Yes, cats, opossums, raccoons, and other night creatures will set them off, but think of it as a sign that the lights are working properly. Understand that motion lights are adjustable. They can stay on for five, ten, or 15 minutes, after the light is tripped. Your choice.)

_____ •Install solar energy lights—that go on at dusk and off at dawn—by exterior doors and bedroom windows.

_____ •Install outside door lights high enough that someone can't reach up and easily unscrew the bulbs.

_____ •Install outside door sconces that totally encase the light bulbs, so they can't be easily broken or unscrewed.

_____ •Use alternating automatic timers to turn your lights, radio, or television on, when you know you're going to be late coming home, or when you're on vacation. The illusion that you are home may deter a break-in. Make it a point to never go home to a completely dark house.

_____ •You may want to secure all possible points of entry with a home security system, that uses either chimes or beeps to alert you when a door or window is opened.

_____ •You may choose to install panic buttons or loud alarms in several places in the house, to alert neighbors of an intruder. Be aware, however, that car alarms generate very little interest, which might also be the case for house alarms, unless you have specifically informed those in your neighborhood. If your immediate neighbors travel a lot, work nights, have a blaring TV, or are heavy sleepers, this may provide another false security in terms of help, although the noise may scare off an intruder.

_____ •Choose a well-known home security system company, or one that has operated in your area for at least five years. (Several companies have moved into my area, and a few months later they are gone.) Make sure the company is qualified, and has the appropriate city and state licenses. Have all of the employees had background checks? Are they all bonded and insured?

_____ •Consider having a central station monitored security alarm installed (experts suggest that the response time should be no more than six minutes).

_____ •Make sure your security system will automatically sound an alarm if your telephone wires are cut. Or have a wireless transmitter installed in your system.

_____ •Conspicuously display the window stickers and the yard signs provided by the alarm system and/or security system services.

_____ •Be alert to strangers and unknown cars on your block. Keep a list of the license numbers. Ask your neighbors to also keep an eye out.

_____ •Plan an escape route, *before* you need one.

_____ •Know the safe spots for taking cover in every room (under tables and desks, behind sofas, and so forth.)

_____ •Look around each room in your house to find items that can be used as improvised weapons—small heavy objects, statues, a cast-iron skillet or griddle, and so on—in case of immediate and unavoidable attack. (Remember when George Harrison and his wife were attacked by a stalker in their home? Olivia cold-cocked the intruder with a table lamp.) Anything can be used. A cheerful, bright red teapot full of sand sits on my stovetop, for just such an occasion. Who would even *think* that its main purpose is to be a potential weapon? Know that wider and heavier items need little accuracy, but can still deliver a powerful blow. Swing, jab, or throw with force. Surprise and determination are key. (I collect rocks, minerals, and crystals of all size, shape, and color. I *love* them. They are placed in every room in my house. I would dislike having to throw these treasures, as I consider them to be Nature's first history books, as well as pieces of art. I also have several thousand books in my home, and I treat them kindly. I would hate to have to throw them at an intruder, but…whatever works!)

_____ •Place your kitchen butcher's block or knife rack out of sight in a cupboard. You don't need to arm an intruder. Know, too, that a knife isn't a good defense weapon, since blade fighting requires a lot of strength, accuracy, and degree of agility that you may not possess. (The movies make it look far too easy!) In addition, even if you manage to stab or slice the aggressor many times, he/she can keep on coming, and continue the attack. Once is not enough; experts maintain that it takes 20 to 30 stabs to disable someone completely. Understand that it will be difficult to fully incapacitate someone with only a knife. (My stalker assaulted and stabbed several women—27 to 37 times each). Remember, the object is to maintain *distance*, not initiate nose-to-nose fighting. However, in a pinch...

_____ •Keep scissors in drawers. Know the location of other small, sharp items (pens, pencils, nail files, letter openers), for jabbing.

_____ •Keep a long tube sock out in the open (in your bedroom, bathroom, or laundry room, where it will be inconspicuous), in which you have placed marbles, or pebbles, or coins, or whatever, to use as a blackjack. Experts suggest, that in a time of haste and need, you can even wrap similar items in a T-shirt, or a pillowslip, for the same affect. Swing it like a bat. Keep swinging!

_____ •Store your aerosol sprays for easy access (hair sprays, deodorant sprays, oven cleaners, spray starch, Lime Away, 409, Shout, and the like), to temporarily blind your attacker. Buy sprays with big handles, and keep the spouts unlocked. Store all such containers at the front of the shelf, facing the back of the cupboard, so they'll always be in the proper position to grab and use. You don't want to accidentally aim it at yourself (which is a problem with pepper spray and mace).

_____ •Is your outside address missing or confusing? Make sure your house number is well lit, and clearly visible from a distance. Replace any dirty, dim, or burned out bulbs immediately. Place the numbers high, prominent, and easy to locate. They must be large enough to be seen from the street, in every kind of weather. Plain numbers are easier to read than fancy numbers, or those written in cursive letters. Numbers are easier and faster to read when placed in a straight line, rather than slanted in descending order. The color of the numbers should stand out vividly from the background. If your numbers are cutouts on a hanging wooden sign, make sure a bright porch light is shining through them. Allow no obstacles (hanging plants, trees, flags, mobiles, banners, art, floral swags, seasonal wreaths, partially opened doors, and the like), to cover or hide any part of the numbers.

_____ •Paint your house numbers with fluorescent paint on your curb (for police, ambulance, and fire personnel). If you live in a rural area, paint your address on both sides of your mailbox.

_____ •Is your front entrance clearly marked? Don't make it a guessing game. If time is of the essence, you won't want emergency personnel on the wrong side of your property, looking for the correct gate or door to enter. Install ground lighting to illuminate the path, or have something that points the way to your front door.

_____ •Any chairs, bicycles, boxes, and such, that you have placed on the porch, should never be allowed to block the doors. Make sure your entrance is clutter free at all times.

_____ •If you have a double front door, make sure that both sides can be easily opened. Do not place a piece of furniture or large plant against one door.

_____ •Never place anything (sports equipment, stacks of boxes) behind your doors, that prevent them from opening flush with the wall. Emergency personnel and their equipment need as much room as possible to gain entrance to any room.

_____ •If you have a mailslot in your door or wall, permanently close it. (A neighbor went away for the weekend, and local children shoved a garden hose through his mailslot, turned the water on, and ran away. You can imagine the state of his wall-to-wall carpet and furniture when he returned.)

_____ •Install a large locking mailbox that is big enough to handle *all* of your incoming mail.

_____ •Do not place your name on the mailbox (your street number or apartment number is sufficient).

_____ •Drop all outgoing mail into a secure U.S. postal service box. It's a pain, but you don't want your payments or important letters stolen.

_____ •If you live in an apartment, with a communal mailbox for larger items, consider renting a private post office box.

_____ •If someone demands your home address, for one reason or another, give him/her the address of your lawyer, with no discussion.

_____ •To better safeguard your address, rent a *retail* post office box, some distance from your house, for all commercial contact. List the box number as a suite or an apartment. Have all official mail, magazines, newsletters, and packages, sent to that box number. Junk mail, like those addressed to "occupant," pleas for donations, and such, would be the only items delivered to your home address.

_____ •Place your post office box on your driver's license, substituting the word suite or apartment, instead of box.

_____ •File a change-of-address form at the post office, giving your private mailbox address.

_____ •Give your new mailing address to all of your friends, requesting that they remove or totally obliterate your old address from their files, Rolodex, and address books.

_____ •Send your new mailing address to all of your creditors, and those you do business with (dentist, doctors, pharmacy, cleaners, bookstores, insurance, tax preparer, cable company, video rental store, et ceterra.)

_____ •Have your name removed from reverse directories.

_____ •Place only your return address on your envelopes, not your name. Do not place your insurance policy numbers on the envelope, even when instructed to do so.

_____ •Experts even suggest that if you have a common name, such as Mary Smith or Tom Jones, that you drop the usage of your middle initial, to further merge with the masses. Your middle initial can help to pinpoint you.

_____ •Make sure that all of your incoming checks—salary warrants, royalties, retirement, income tax, et cetera—are Direct Deposit. (My son had two checks stolen from his mailbox, the recovery of which was difficult and time-consuming.)

_____ •If an unexpected package is found on your doorstep, do not touch it. Check the postmark to see if it matches the return address. If you didn't order anything, or don't recognize the sender, or it doesn't have a return address that is clearly legible, get to safety, and call 911. (I was constantly finding packages that were made to look like they had been delivered through the U.S. mail, but they were always left on my porch far too early to have been legitimate. Thank goodness they held only perfume, and not anything gross or deadly.)

_____ •Handle unusual or unexpected mail with care. Touch them around the envelope edges, leaving as few smudges and fingerprints as possible.

_____ •Place threatening mail in Ziploc bags. Include the envelopes, even if torn.

_____ •Do not write on the original mail. (Xerox copies on which to make notations, and record the date received. Although Post-It notes will not damage the evidence, they can easily get lost.) Do not staple or tape the material.

_____ •Shred or destroy all discarded mail. (My brother's office and home trashcans were inspected for six weeks—by business competitors—before he figured it out, which turned out to be a very costly experience). Buy a shredder that turns your paper into confetti.

_____ •Become friendly with your neighborhood mail carrier. (Bob, our postman, knows everyone on his route. He keeps an eye on the elderly who live alone, and notices potential safety hazards in the area, and alerts neighbors as need be. He's like a member of eveyone's family.) Inform your postal carrier of your stalking situation. He/she is in a good position to spot any strangers, unrecognized vehicles, or suspicious activity. The more eyes watching out for you, the better.

_____ •Lock your outside electrical, breaker, and fuse boxes to prevent tampering.

_____ •Keep heavy-duty flashlights on hand, with fresh batteries.

_____ •Keep a battery-operated lantern on hand, with fresh batteries.

_____ •Keep candles on hand, with matches nearby.

_____ •Install smoke detectors in various rooms, and on each floor. Check them yearly (at daylight savings time).

_____ •Keep a first aid kit on each floor.

_____ •Keep a fire extinguisher handy, on each floor. Know how to use them.

_____ •Use baking soda to put out small kitchen fires. Sand will also have the same effect. (Remember my little red teapot full of sand? It really serves a dual purpose.)

_____ •Install phones throughout the house, on two separate lines. If your intruder disables one phone, he/she probably won't think that there is another line. (I had a second line installed, strictly for my teenagers to use. It made my life considerably easier.)

_____ •Do not install your phones next to windows. Besides making it easy for your conversations to be overheard, a stalker will know where you are, when you answer your phone.

_____ •Consider changing your phone number. Make sure that your phone number is unpublished and unlisted. (I never changed my number, even though my stalker knew it, simply because I preferred to have my stalker at the end of the phone line, than on my front porch. Of course, this was before cell phones. Things are different now.) Have the bill sent to your mailbox address.

_____ •Do the same with your cell phone, having the bill sent to your retail mailbox, and place a password on the account.

_____ •Keep a whistle or an airhorn next to the phone, to blow into the ear of lewd and offensive callers, or silent listeners, until you get an answering machine. (This tactic certainly discouraged some of my callers in past years.)

_____ •Buy and install an answering machine.

_____ •Know that your own recorded message on your answering machine may reward your stalker. (Some have been known to call up to 60 times a day, just to hear their target's voice.) Have someone of the opposite sex record your outgoing generic message. Make it short, *without* including your name, phone number, schedule, or any other information. If you are single, use the word "we" regardless, leaving the caller unsure of how many people may be living with you. (Something akin to: "We're unable to take your call at the moment" or, "We'll get back to you" or even a no nonsense, "Leave your name" or "State your business.") Your family and friends will understand your situation, and won't take offense. Better yet, use an impersonal electronic voice that simply instructs the caller to leave a message.

_____ •Consider having a vicious dog growling or barking in the background while you are giving your message.

_____ •Never leave chatty messages on your answering machine, saying that you are working late, or are going on vacation for a week. That simply invites burglars.

_____ •Use the answering machine to screen your calls. Remember: the phone is for *your* convenience, not the caller's.

_____ •Keep *all* answering machine tapes of your stalker's calls, not just the threatening messages. Date them immediately.

_____ •Or use an answering service.

_____ •Add a Caller ID devise (but know upfront that if your stalker or harasser is calling from outside your area code, the display panel will not record. Which is also the problem with a Star 57 call trace. Understand, too, that if his/her service is blocked, the display panel will read "Anonymous." The terms "Unavailable" or "Not Available" mean that the call is either from a cell phone, a telemarketer, or your phone company's competitor's pay phone, and the number will not be captured). As such, Caller ID may be rather useless, unless people you *do* wish to speak with call at an inconvenient time, or when you are out, and you want to return their calls later.

_____ •Another optional residential phone service, Call Intercept, is now available insome areas. It lets you avoid strangers, and stop those unwanted callers that normally show up as "private," "out of the area," "unavailable," or "anonymous" on your Caller ID box. This service asks those callers to record their names before your phone rings. When you answer, you hear the recording, so you can decide whether to take the call or not. Or, you can forward it to Home Voice Mail. If callers refuse to give their names, they are disconnected before your phone even rings.

_____ •Home Voice Mail answers your calls for you, so you won't miss important calls, but can ignore the rest. You can even check your messages from another location.

_____ •Keep emergency numbers by all telephones.

_____ •Understand that cordless or cellular phones are essentially radio transmitters. Never discuss any personal information when using one, as special electrical equipment can illegally listen to your "private" conversations. (A neighbor used a walkie-talkie, and it interfered with my phone conversations. I could hear everything he and his buddies were saying.)

_____ •Experts suggest that you not call an 800, 877, 888, or 900 line from your home phone. Although it's an inconvenience, use a public phone. Even if you have a Blocking service, those numbers are captured, recorded, and stored by the owners of those lines, which are then available to anyone with access to that database. In addition, it will also appear on the called party's bill.

_____ •It is also suggested that your relatives and close friends, who live a long distance from you, should likewise use a pay phone to contact you. An Automatic Number Identification devise records the caller's name and telephone number, giving others easy access to *their* addresses.

_____ •Never give out personal information over the phone to a pollster or a solicitor (especially not your social security number, mother's maiden name, or your bank or credit account numbers). If the company, bank, or charity is credible, deal with them through the mail or in person. Never conduct business over the phone.

_____ •Never verify your address over the phone to your bank or catalog companies.

_____ •Experts insist that *no* Internet transaction is private, regardless of who says otherwise. Your information passes through a number of computers (which can capture and store the data) before arriving at the intended destination, and there are illegal devices sold that can access such information.

_____ •Keep the above in mind: To discourage those other annoying and harassing phone calls from telemarketers, the government suggests that you can block at least 80 percent of their calls by signing up on the national DO NOT CALL list. (According to the FCC, telemarketers attempt up to 104 million calls to consumers every day.) You can sign up for the registry on the Web site, **www.donotcall.gov**, or call the toll-free number **(888) 382-1222** (from the phone or cell phone you wish to register). Consider, however, that you will be on yet another list.

_____ •Understand that each and every time you post a message to a chat room, or a discussion group, or forward jokes, cartoons, and silly sayings, you are putting your address on the Internet where it's available for anyone to copy and use. Tell your friends not to forward your e-mails to someone else (who may forward them to someone else, and so on).

_____ •Since there is no way to remove your e-mail address from search engines, you may want to switch to a different account (which you will *never* post online). Or, so experts tell us, if you want to continue using chat rooms and discussion groups, you should go to sites like Yahoo and Hotmail and create a secondary e-mail account.

_____ •When using an ATM, shield the keypad when entering your PIN, and make sure you take your transaction receipt with you. Shred it before throwing it away.

_____ •Promptly review your bank and credit card statements for unauthorized activity.

_____ •Don't preprint your driver's license or Social Security numbers on your checks.

_____ •Experts suggest that you order checks through your bank, as it may have extra security features built into both the checks and the ordering procedure.

_____ •When you receive a new shipment of checks, make sure your order is complete.

_____ •Store your birth certificate and your Social Security card in your safety deposit box.

_____ •Safeguard your social security number and your mother's maiden name. Anyone can access your accounts with such information and easily obtain your address, or steal your identity. Never allow such information on any public record.

_____ •You already have many records with your social security number and mother's maiden name already on them. Find those documents, and close them to public view.

_____ •Shred your old documents that have personal information listed on them.

_____ •Experts suggest that you consider substituting the social security number 078-05-1120 in place of yours, for those organizations who demand one, but have no legal reason to do so. (It's an old sample number, which was never assigned to anyone.) Using that number is certainly easier than arguing with bean-counting bureaucrats. Other available numbers range from 987-65-4320 through 4329. Pick one. If neither the IRS nor Social Security cares that you use the number for unreasonable requests, why should you?

_____ •Do not fill out warranty cards (you *still* have the warranty if you keep the receipt). Likewise, do not fill out surveys, contest, or sweepstakes entry forms. The information therein is sold to many parties. The same holds true for product, coupon, and free sample questionnaires. Nothing is for free.

_____ •Understand that if you subscribe to magazines, or newspapers at your residential address, your address will be recorded in a database, for easy access. Use your P.O. Box address, or buy them at the stands.

_____ •Consider whether you want your personal information to be included in the databases of professional associations, service organizations, club memberships, charities, and the like. (I am a member of over 50 widely diverse groups—education, library, writing, anticensorship, environment/conservation, and women's groups, et cetera, local, national, and international. I can't even imagine how many lists include my name, address, phone number, and other data. The mind boggles.)

_____ •Understand that any school you attended also has your personal information. High school, college, and university reunion committees know a lot about you. It may be wise not to divulge the names of your alma maters.

_____ •Some service clubs—like our local Lions Club—print the entire memberships' information on their biweekly newsletter: full name, spouse's name, birthdays, addresses, business, and phone numbers. It becomes a matter of convenience versus privacy. What if a newsletter falls into the wrong hands?

_____ •Do not place your personal information at your place of worship.

_____ •Consider giving cash or anonymous money orders to charities and political organizations, rather than having your information on even more databanks. An added incentive to this idea is that you will no longer have to deal with the crush of mail asking for further donations from similar groups. (From the amount of uninvited, unexpected, and unwanted mail I receive on a daily basis, it is clear that my personal information has been sold numerous times.)

_____ •Inform your utilities and credit card companies that you need to encode your account with a password. (Do not choose an obvious word!) Specialists suggest that after several weeks, call to access your account. Did anyone ask you for your password? If not, speak to the supervisor *and* write to the company. (Letters carry more clout, but phones are more immediate.) Your privacy is essential.

_____ •A disturbing trend is evident in some retail stores: Even when paying *cash* at checkout counters, clerks ask for home addresses and/or e-mail addresses. (I am amazed at the number of customers that automatically respond—while dozens of people are within hearing distance—without thinking of the consequences.) Refuse to give out personal information to anyone without a legitimate need to know.

_____ •Have your driver's license and vehicle registration address also listed at the distant retail mailbox address.

_____ •Keep your personal information out of public records. To see what records are open for public inspection, check out the privacy laws on the Internet, for your state, such as **www.privacyprotection.ca.gov** or **www.privacyrights.org/fs/fs11-pub.htm** (Although California laws currently cover 19 privacy-related subjects, be advised that they do not necessarily afford a great deal of privacy *protection*.)

_____ •Hire a lawyer to get any past or current court records sealed.

_____ •Get periodic reports from the major credit bureaus—Experian, Equifax, and TransUnion—to ensure that your private information is not being released. (I recently received two letters, in one week, from loan companies. Both listed the exact balance on my credit card accounts, and inquired as to whether I'd like to borrow money to pay them off. I was not happy to hear that *any* company can pay to get such credit information, which includes your full name, address, marital status, work history, and such.) Pay off your credit cards and close the accounts. Cash is safer. (**Equifax: 1-888-766-0008; Experian: 1-888-397-3742; TransUnion: 1-800-680-7289**)

_____ •The above-listed agencies will also place an alert on your file, if you're a victim of account or identity theft. They can also assist in the investigation.

_____ •The Federal Trade Commission (FTC) has a database with information and complaints associated with identity theft. Victims of identity theft can contact the FTC at **1-877-438-4338**, or on the Internet at **www.consumer.gov/idtheft**.

_____ •If your house has a second floor, secure flame resistant emergency escape ladders near windows and/or balconies.

_____ •Always store your pepper spray or firearms where you can obtain them quickly, but out of the reach of children.

_____ •If you live in a gated apartment, make sure that residents are aware of your potential problem, and that they are *never* to hold the outside doors or gates open for people they don't know. Have particulars listed in the tenant's newsletter, or discussed in a condo owner's meeting, and/or posted.

_____ •Never allow your name to be listed on a building directory.

_____ •If you live in an apartment, make sure that your intercom is working at all times. (Remember Rebecca Schaeffer.)

_____ •If you live in a guarded community, make sure that your name is red-flagged, so those who are manning the entrance kiosk will not give out any information about you, including the fact that you live there. Give them a flyer (with a photo and physical description of your stalker). Instruct them to call the police if he/she tries to enter the premises, and to inform you, as well.

_____ •Avoid being in an apartment laundry room at night by yourself. (A close friend was raped in her apartment laundry room one night, in what was considered to be a safe and secure building. The man was never caught.) On average, a rapist will rape 17 different women before being tracked, arrested, charged, tried, convicted, and sentenced, only to serve a short amount of time in jail or prison. They are more than likely be paroled first—sex offenders being considered non-violent—while the recidivism rate is 80 percent. Research shows that less than one in ten rapes are reported to the police, so don't fail to report such an experience. Rapists need to be off the streets!

_____ •Never leave a note on your door or mailbox. That's simply an invitation for your house to be burgled or vandalized.

_____ •Upon returning home, if you find a broken window, an open or unlocked door, or things look slightly askew, do not enter the premises. If you smell perfume, aftershave, or cigarette smoke that shouldn't be there, or hear what sounds like floor or stair creaks, or you see a slight shadow, do not step indoors. If something doesn't feel quite right, a shiver goes up your spine, or the hair goes up your arms, heed your intuition! Backtrack and call 911. Wait for the police to check it out, as an intruder may still be lurking therein.

_____ •Sometimes stalkers enjoy being in your home—in your own personal space—and will move things around, or take items, or leave something behind, just to play around with your mind. (I was once a guest on the "IN PERSON with Maureen O'Boyle" show about Stalking. One of the other guests said that her clothes were often moved around in her closet; and that once, when she had laid out an outfit for the next day, she returned later to find a completely different outfit laid out on her bed. It was later found that the guy lived upstairs, directly over her apartment. Locally, a stalker stole his victim's panties, and hung them his garage.)

_____ •If things seem to be missing, or seem to be shuffled around—but you're really not *sure*—you may want to invest in a sound-activated tape recorder, or place a camouflaged video recorder, hidden inside a clock, a teddy bear, whatever, in the room of your choice.

_____ •Make it difficult for an intruder to hide. When you go out, leave your closet doors wide open, so you'll instantly know if someone is hiding therein. (You might also want to install closet lights.) Raise your floor-length tablecloths so no one can hide under dining or end tables or bed tables. Pull up your dust ruffles, or have your bedframes sit closer to the floor, so you are assured that no one is under the beds. If your bed sits high, extend the head, foot, and sideboards lower to the ground, for the same affect. Place trundle beds under your children's beds.

_____ •A single friend keeps finding a specific brand of candy wrappers left on her property at night, that her stalker is known to favor. She is certain that he leaves them as calling cards, to let her know that he's watching her. Since the police told her that any number of people could be in her backyard leaving the candy wrappers, she is saving money for a nightscope video camera, to prove that he's the culprit. But the expense is prohibitive, being that she is handicapped and on a limited income. It's been suggested that she try to rent one for the short-term, to see if she gets any results, or to shop at pawn shops to see if she could get a nightscope video camera there, for less. Check it out, if you have a similar situation.

_____ •Request periodic police drivebys of your residence.

_____ •Alone in a house at night, people feel the most vulnerable while taking a bath. If possible, change your schedule to an earlier bath.

_____ •Consider turning your master bathroom into a Safe Room. Install a second pocket door, or a solid-core or steel door with a deadbolt lock (or a Door Jammer if you're in an apartment). If you have children, however, you may want to use the baby's room, or the youngest child's room, as a Safe Room, since it will be easier for you (and older children) to go there, than to try to awaken and carry a child back to your bathroom. Also, consider the window factor when choosing a Safe Room. You don't want to choose a room in which a window could be easily smashed to gain entrance. Keep a phone, candles or a lantern with matches, as well as packaged dried fruit, crackers, and bottled water, stored therein, in case of a lengthy wait. Stay put until the police arrive.

_____ •Of course, if money is no object, then you may be a target for kidnappers. (One such family has a hidden Safe Room on all three floors of their house, as well as a separate hidden staircase connecting all floors. The rooms are large enough to accommodate a number of people, with proper ventilation and supplies, along with a safe, guns, a CB radio, a battery-operated portable radio, a panic button wired directly into the police department, and video monitors of the house and extensive property. There is no way anyone could break through the doors, even if they could actually *find* the Safe Rooms).

_____ •Besides being concerned about stalkers, rapists, and burglars, there are those who worry about civil unrest. (Another family I know has a tunnel extending from under their house to the far edge of their property, in addition to a hidden Safe Room).

_____ •If a stalker or intruder has broken into your home while you are there, and silence is an issue, know that you can dial 911 and simply leave the phone off the hook, and the police are required to check out the circumstances.

_____ •Identify and record your property in case of robbery, vandalism, or fire. Use an engraving pen to mark your Social Security number or your Driver's License number—along with your state initials—on each item. Videotape all rooms by standing in the middle of each room and slowing panning the interior. Don't depend on your memory (a decade after our house fire, we're *still* remembering things that were lost). Experts suggest that you photograph all your jewelry, fine art, and antiques, alongside your actual Driver's License or your Social Security card.

_____ •Some police departments offer free home inspections. Call them for information, or to make an appointment.

_____ •Of course, another layer of defense is to surround your property with sturdy fences or high walls. (For years, the bulk of my income was invested in art. Every place I've lived, my apartment or house was broken into, because it wasn't completely surrounded by a fence or wall. Only small items were taken, showing the perpetrators to be those in need of enough money for a daily fix. Luckily, my art collection was never touched, showing that the thieves didn't know what they were looking at, or couldn't afford the time, effort, and energy to take a large and heavy painting or sculpture, and maneuver it outside without causing suspicion. They would have been far too conspicuous hauling such property out of the front door.)

_____ •Add electric security gates, with a time-release mechanism, automatically closing within a few seconds of your entry. Such gates won't completely deter determined intruders, but burglars know they can't steal large items. (At one school where I taught, a teacher was raped in her classroom, before school began, by two men. They had pulled their car up to her bungalow—as the children played on the playground—parking crosswise in front of the steps, so no one could enter. One man waited in the driver's seat, while the other did his business, and then they changed places. As a result, the huge school was later surrounded by a 10-foot-high chainlink fence, as a security measure. Unfortunately, no gates were installed, leaving the school in no better shape than it was, beforehand, since the opening was large enough to drive two huge trash trucks in, side-by-side. It was a cosmetic approach to safety; something to reassure the public, while doing nothing to sooth or alleviate the teachers' rattled nerves.)

_____ •Move, only as a last resort. Know at the outset that moving without leaving a paper trail is extremely difficult. (For instance, if you use a moving van that has the company name spread across its sides, you've lost before you've begun.) Understand, too, that isolation is not protection. When considering a residential move, carefully weigh the pros and cons of such a decision. If money is no problem, of course, that makes it easier for you. Even so, consider whether you may feel separated and apart from your new neighbors (who don't know you, and may not *care* about your problems, or may *resent* the fact that you've placed them in a potentially dangerous situation). Know up front that you might be sacrificing much needed help and support from those who have a neighborhood history with you. And, if you have children, that only complicates the issue: Will it be easy to change their names? Schools? Friends? Can they keep secrets? Can they be easily tricked into revealing information? Know in advance that it won't be easy. Also, keep in mind that privacy is a problem in this day and age. (I have a friend that moved *nine* times in one year, and her ex-husband still found her, and slit her throat. Luckily she survived, although she now talks in a low, raspy voice. She presently teaches self-defense to women, and offers deaf and disabled services at LACAAW; A woman I counseled moved all the way to California from Tennessee to get away from her ex-husband, and he was still able to find her. Because she felt that her daughter's life was also at stake, she moved again, and I lost track of her for several years. She recently wrote me a letter saying that they had moved back into the area, and both she and her daughter were doing well.) Realize, too, that the most difficult and daunting part of this kind of move is that you must completely change your old lifestyle habits and comfortable routines (gyms, classes, clubs, hobbies, sports, banking, jogging, bicycling, pets, movies, et cetera), or you can easily be found again. (One woman was tracked down via veterinary services.) In addition, it's not wise to use your charge cards. Unless you have only a few personal items, know that a secret move requires *extensive* thought and planning on your part. And you must *never* return to retrieve personal items left behind. (Having said that, however, I do know women that have moved successfully, so it *can* be accomplished.) In the end, it boils down to your decision to balance the need for physical safety with the loss of supportive relationships and familiar surroundings.

_____ •If you move into an apartment or condominium, know that the higher the floor, the less likely an intruder can enter through your windows.

_____ •California has a Safe at Home confidential address program that allows stalking victims to have their addresses, DMV, and voter information kept confidential. All bills, checks, and mail of any kind are sent to Sacramento, and then returned to the addressee's confidential address (**1-877-322-5227** or **www.so.ca.gov/safeathome/**). Check your state to see if it has a similar program in effect. (A friend says that this program has given her peace of mind.)

_____ •Experts suggest that if you've recently moved, refrain from voting (Eeek!) for the time being, until you make arrangements for your voter information to be kept secret. (Yet another freedom taken away by a stalker.)

_____ •If you're moving a distance away, you may also consider changing your name, as well as those of your children (somewhat like the witness protection program). Think of it as your *stage* name or alias. (The beauty parlor that I patronize had six beauticians with the same first name: Mary. So five go by their middle names, and one uses a shortened form of her last name. It works for them.)

_____ •Know that you can have new social security numbers listed for yourself and your children, if you can show evidence of your being abused, harassed, or stalked (police or medical reports, restraining orders, shelter or counselor's letters, et cetera). You need also bring birth certificates, driver's license, and proof that you are the parent, and/or have legal custody of the children. Check with the Social Security Administration at **www.ssa.gov** for particulars.

_____ •Consider placing your rental agreement in another name (a nonexistent roommate or a fictional significant other).

_____ •Consider transferring the title of any new property to a close relative, or an old and trusted friend (Make sure! I could tell you stories…), or your privately owned business, or a trust, as the county assessor, county recorder, and business license information is public. Consult a lawyer in any case. All a stalker has to do is call the county assessor's office to receive your residential address.

_____ •Experts also suggest that if you relocate, that you trade in your car, for a different one, with different license plates.

_____ •If in a new location, contact family and friends through public phones. Never Tell anyone where you are.

_____ •Understand that your finances will be seriously impacted over the long haul. It's not fair, but that's the reality of the situation. Make a long-range plan, and buy or save toward whatever security items you can afford, each month. Deal with it. Just knowing that you have a way to upgrade your safety will set your mind at ease. Be confident that you are improving your situation. Take charge.

FAMILY SAFETY

_____ •Commit to improving your family's safety. Design a safety plan to suit your family's needs. You'll feel more at ease, knowing that you've done as much as you can to take care of all your family members.

_____ •Make sure that your whole family understands the seriousness of the situation. Do not expect children to remember new procedures, after having been told the new rules only once or twice. Practice and review often. To cut down the anxiety, make a game out of knowing the answers.

_____ •Ensure that all family members regularly trade information about unusual or suspicious activities, or anything even slightly out of the ordinary.

_____ •Plan house evacuation drills with *all* those family members living with you. Make sure they know multiple exits for emergency situations, and where to meet, and what to do, afterwards. Practice every month, just like schools do with fire drills.

_____ •Make sure young children know their full names and address, as well as your name (not mommy or daddy). "We live in a big yellow house," is not going to help rescue services.

_____ *Educate your young children in the use of making a 911 call.

_____ •Stress that your children do *not* answer the phone. Depend on Caller ID for identification and the answering machine for messages. They are *never* to say that they are alone, or tell others where *you* may be.

_____ •Make sure that an adult family member always knows your schedule, and amended plans, concerning your whereabouts.

_____ •It is imperative that you always know the schedule of each child in your family. If their plans change unexpectedly, have a safe house ready to accommodate them, until you can arrive.

_____ •You must have a thorough background check completed, and references read, *before* you hire a babysitter, house cleaner, cook, gardener, driver, or handyman. (We had just moved into a new apartment complex, and I was in a bind, needing a babysitter fast. I asked a group of my new neighbors if they could recommend anyone. One woman offered her services on the spot. I was so happy, and relieved to have a sitter close at hand. Late that night, five different women, separately, knocked on my door, urging me not to use this particular babysitter. It turned out that the woman's husband was a batterer, and had already put both of their young sons in the hospital. This was in the days before people were arrested for domestic abuse. Needless to say, I found another sitter.)

_____ •Make sure that your children, babysitter, or house cleaner do not answer the door, even when you are in the house. They are *never* to let a stranger in the house, for any reason, under any circumstances.

_____ •Either drive your children to school, or walk with them, or wait with them at the bus stop. If you can't personally do so, make arrangements for another adult, or a trusted older adolescent, to be present with them.

_____ •Obtain a copy of each of your children's school's safety policies, especially if both public and private schools are involved, or if different districts are utilized, or if you are dealing with elementary, middle, and high schools. They may all differ.

_____ •Inform your children's school administrators, teachers, and coaches of the potential stalking problem. Give them all the pertinent information. Make it clear to all school personnel that they are never to allow your children to be picked up by anyone other than designated family members. Make sure that you have recorded specific family names that are placed on record in the school office, for pick-up purposes. (Write down *several* names, just in case your primary choices are unavailable when needed). In the event that no one shows to collect your children, know that school office personnel will take care of them. And, if you do not arrive at an acceptable time, they can sound the alarm for you. Both of which should relieve your mind.

_____ •Caution your children to travel in-groups.

_____ •Do not have the children's names displayed on their clothing or backpacks. A stalker, kidnapper, or pedophile can then call the child's name—feigning that he/she knows the family—momentarily disarming the child's natural suspicions.

_____ •Vary your routine even with your children. Although you can't change the hours of school, club meetings, scheduled practices, or sporting events, you *can* change when you arrive, how you arrive, the route you take to get there, and where you park, as well as the route you take home.

_____ •Be aware of new faces, and anyone who appears to be loitering, or simply looks out of place around schools, practice grounds, or sporting events.

_____ •Report any suspicious strangers or behavior immediately. Inform several people, in case one person gets distracted and forgets to follow through.

_____ •Give each child a cellular phone or personal alarm.

_____ •Consider having your children take some form of self-defense class that promotes boundary setting alongside that of verbal and physical techniques (hitting, kicking, or scratching targeted areas). You don't want your child just flailing around, being ineffective. They need to respond with knowledge.

_____ •If unavailable in your area, try martial arts classes. If nothing else, it will strengthen their self-confidence, perseverance, and respect, while getting a good dose of hard work and exercise.

_____ •Know that both children and adults are stalked prior to being abducted.

_____ •Children must understand that no adult needs help from a child. Although youngsters will want to help—especially upon hearing that an animal is involved—tell them that if they hear the words, "Can you help me find my lost puppy?" or "Can you help me find my lost kitten?" they are to *run* away as fast as possible. (When I was around six years old, I was browsing in a five-and-dimestore, looking at the valentine displays. A grandfatherly man came up to me, asking if I would come to the back of the store, and help him pick out a dinner plate pattern, so he could buy the set for his wife. I thought it strange that he would ask me, since I had never paid the slightest attention to plate designs beforehand. Even though this was in the days long before anyone ever talked about the dangers of strangers, I instinctively knew that he had an ulterior motive, although I couldn't fathom what that might be. It just didn't make sense to me that he would want a little girl to choose a pattern for a grown woman. I also noted the fact that there was a wide-open door on the side wall, close to the back of the building, adjacent to the plate display, and the area appeared darker— ominous, somehow—and nobody else was in that section, which also spooked me, for some reason. The whole situation was just too weird. And although I politely told him no several times (afterall, he was an elder), and walked away, he was insistent, following me around the store. I finally gave in, rushed to the back of the store, pointed at the first set of plates that I saw, and then ran back and plunged into the middle of the crowd buying valentines. I ended up hiding behind a counter, even though I didn't know *why* I was so afraid. I didn't have the understanding, much less the words, to explain any of this to my parents. So I never said anything. It gives me the creeps now, just thinking about it.) Talk with your children, making sure they understand that if an adult needs help with *any*thing, they will ask another adult, not a child.

_____ •Children also need to understand that if a stranger offers them candy, ice cream, sodas, or presents, they are to *run* away immediately. (One of the students in anelementary school in which I taught, was lured by *quarters* for video games, and abducted. The boy was found two years later in New York City, with the same pedophile. Statistics clearly show that the longer a person is missing, the smaller the chance of recovery, so this boy was lucky to be found—completely across the country— much less, found alive!)

_____ •Educate your children on the importance of an *immediate* and strong resistance to kidnapping: screaming, fighting, running away, yelling ("Help! I need help! I don't know him/her!"), and making a loud commotion. They must know that they are *never, ever* to get in a vehicle of someone they don't know. They must kick, scratch, pull hair, and anything else they can do to avoid it. If they are overpowered, and forced into a car or van, they must use their brains to figure out a way to escape or attract attention in any way whatsoever.

_____ •Teach your children that not *all* strangers are bad. If they are in need of help, almost *anyone* will help a child. They are to look for mothers with children, or crossing guards, postal carriers, city workmen, et cetera.

_____ •Discuss the situation with your children, role-play with them, and enroll them in child safety programs. Suggest that their schools support schoolwide safety programs.

_____ •If another student is stalking your child, or engaging in behavior that is a known precursor to stalking, get the school involved right away. The sooner this behavior is nipped in the bud, the better. With a safety issue at hand, and a possible liability problem in the offing, administrators have several options to persue: suspension and/or transfer, or expulsion. (With only around six weeks left of his senior year, the *valedictorian* of the high school flipped out, when his girlfriend broke off their relationship. His resultant behavior was so off-the-wall, as well as dangerous, that he was *expelled*. So much for his college plans).

_____ •Use as many nightlights as necessary, not only to make your house safe, but to make it *feel* safe for your children.

_____ •Beware of pedophiles using the Internet. Educate your family concerning the net. Make sure that your children understand that they are *never* to respond to inappropriate communications. They must immediately log off, or find a more suitable site. Know where your children intend to surf.

_____ •Buy and use software that can block access to unsuitable chat rooms.

_____ •Be aware that your spouse or significant other may be unable to cope with the relentless, unexpected disruptions, and loss of control, feeling a sense of impotence regarding your stalking situation. He/she may desperately want to help you, but can't in a meaningful way, and may feel frustrated and depressed because of the inability to make things better or easier for you. Your partner may take steps to emotionally distance him/herself from you. As such, you may feel not only a lack of support, but also a sense of withdrawal, whenever unwanted letters, packages, phone calls, or the police are in evidence. It's like positive proof that your partner is in position of weakness or helplessness; one in which he/she can't "protect" you or "save" you. It has a demoralizing affect. Many partners are unable to deal with the constant worry and stress of a stalker, and, coupled with a lowered self-esteem, are unable to deal with the crisis adequately. It can definitely put a strain on your present relationships. Many partners opt out completely.

_____ •In addition, children and young teens may also become selfish, and a tad jealous, if you seem to be constantly preoccupied with a "phantom" stalker. They want your time, efforts, energy, and thought focused in their direction. They have no concept of the stress and strain that you are under. Don't expect them to understand what you are going through. They can't. Reassure your children of your love, and give them your attention. Worry on your own time.

_____ •If your ex-spouse is stalking you—and you had children together—and a court has ordered visitation rights, do not meet face-to-face with him/her, even if it is in a public place. If your stalker is bent upon harming you, he/she would just as soon have witnesses to the crime, than not. This would be a perfect time and place to gain the attention your stalker craves: his/her 15 minutes of fame. Have a third party handle the drop offs and pick ups.

SOCIAL SAFETY

_____ •Commit to improving your social safety skills by choosing to live more carefully. Crime and violence is a fact of life. (A woman now has a one in four chance of experiencing a violent crime in her lifetime.) The statistics are horrible, even though they are vastly underreported and underrepresented. Educate yourself regarding prevention procedures, self-protection, and survival techniques.

_____ •Don't assume that just because you meet someone new at the house of a friend, or a semi-private gathering, that the host vouches for the stranger's character. This person may be only a dim or distant acquaintance, or simply a friend of a friend of a friend, or may have even crashed the event. Do not attach the host's qualities to that of the stranger.

_____ •Never leave your purse, personal planner, or briefcase unattended. Don't leave them in a back room, or closet, unsupervised, at a gathering or meeting. (My brother's entire personal planner was photocopied—along with the addresses and phone numbers of all his business contacts—which turned out to be very costly). At a party or an event in which some strangers will be in attendance, bring only what is necessary. Lock your belongings in the trunk of your car, or leave them at home.

_____ •Always leave large gatherings, meetings, or parties in a group.

_____ •Be wary of a stranger who stands too close, invading your space; be mindful of anyone who stares at you, or asks personal questions regarding your home situation.

_____ •Cultivate a don't-mess-with-me attitude.

_____ •Do not convey distraction. Understand that the way you carry yourself says volumes. Walk with assurance, and with purpose. Determine to appear confident, wherever you are. Hold your back straight, your head high, and give eye contact.

_____ •Never discount or disregard your intuition. Respect your gut reactions. Your intuition is a built-in resource. Use it.

_____ •Understand that *anyone* can be a tracker—men, women, and children. Look for a person that you see more than once in a crowd. (While in a mall, late one evening, I took notice of a man several times, who seemed out of place. He was elderly, and wearing a white suit. I overrode my instincts by telling myself that a "grandfather" in such a distinctive outfit could never pose a threat. Sadly, he followed me out into the deserted parking lot, exposed himself, and ejaculated all over the car.)

_____ •Don't ignore the odd or unusual. (In a hurry, as I parked in a lot late one afternoon, I noticed a young man in a trench coat, pacing back and forth in front of the large grocery store, checking his watch. I assumed that he was impatiently waiting for a girlfriend. Even so, his outfit seemed out of place, as this was sunny, Southern California, and I had always pictured long overcoats to be a New York style. So I decided that he was a visitor. Charging into the grocery store on the run, I noted the startled reaction of the young man as I whizzed by, and he turned and followed me inside. To make a long story short, I had stumbled into a robbery in progress. It turned out that all five gang members wore trench coats, under which they had hidden shotguns.) Make the connections.

_____ •Be discreet. Never give casual acquaintances—not to mention strangers—personal information about yourself. Keep your small talk small.

_____ •Do not display the numbers on your cellular phone or pager. It is possible to get your name and address from your numbers.

_____ •Watch what you say on a cell phone when out in public. Both important and private conversations can be overheard by anyone within listening range. (I've heard people talking *loudly* on their cell phones while in the mall, grocery stores, theaters, restaurants, bars, and casinos, as well as classrooms, weddings and funerals.) Besides being rude to other people in the vicinity, eavesdroppers can do some damage with just a few of the personal facts being bandied about. Con artists, intruders, and robbers relish such unsolicited information.

_____ •Make sure you tell family members or friends about each new acquaintance that has come into your life.

_____ •Meet new dates at several populated spots *before* handing out your home address. Exercise caution.

_____ •Especially let others know about each new date *before* you go out with him/her, as well as the intended site and location (restaurant, movie, dance). In addition, *post* such information on your refrigerator, or message board, as well. No exceptions.

_____ •Inform your friends and neighbors of your stalking situation. Update them, as needed. Do not suffer in silence. Talk, talk, talk. Let everyone know.

_____ •Make sure that your Neighborhood Watch knows about your stalking problem. The more eyes and ears, the better.

_____ •Make flyers including your stalker's name and description (ethnicity, age and birthdate, if known, height, weight, color of eyes and hair, and any permanent identifiers: scars, birthmarks, tattoos, accent, et cetera), with information regarding his/her car description and license plate number. Include a photograph, if possible. Place them in your neighbor's mailboxes. Keep a stack handy. Pass them out, as needed. (Youngsters delivered 400 flyers for me.) Give one to your doorman if you live in a secured apartment or a gated community.

_____ •Always do your gym workouts with a buddy. Always go walking, jogging, or biking with a friend, or not at all.

_____ •Never go walking, jogging, biking, or use outside tennis courts at night, even with a friend.

_____ •When going for a walk or a run, tuck your key, ID, and a few bills into the zippered compartment of your sock, ankle/arm wallet, or fannypack. Or simply tie your key to your shoelace bow. Always keep your hands free.

_____ •Never wear earphones when walking, jogging, or biking. They cut off a survival sense that can warn you of approaching danger. If you can't do without music or your tape, at least keep one ear free. Your awareness needs to extend in all directions at all times.

_____ •Experts suggest that you carry pepper spray or a mini-baton when walking or jogging. Understand that such tools are not useful if stored in your fanny pack, backpack, or purse. They must be in a ready-to-use position.

_____ •Consider carrying an umbrella or a cane while shopping, to extend your personal boundary. Again, keep in mind that either can be taken and used against you.

_____ •Keep your cell phone handy in a pocket or fanny pack, when out and about.

_____ •Always face oncoming traffic when walking, jogging, or biking.

_____ •If a vehicle stops (presumably for information or directions), keep on moving. Don't become a stationary target.

_____ •If a vehicle appears to be following you, move to the other side of the street. If it turns around in your direction, head for safety immediately.

_____ •If friends drive you home, have them wait until you enter your house, before they leave.

_____ •Know that elevators are considered to be the most unsafe areas in public facilities. If a stranger makes you the least bit nervous or ill at ease, elect to wait for the next elevator, or consider taking the stairs. If in an elevator, and someone enters on another floor that makes you uncomfortable, get off and walk away with purpose. Wait a while, then double back and take another one.

_____ •Stay alert. An elevator is not the place to read a map or brochure, flip through your mail, clean your glasses, or distractedly fish around in your pockets or purse. Without being obvious about it, keep your eye on strangers.

_____ •While riding in an elevator, stand with your back against the wall, and close to the control panel. Hit the alarm button if necessary. (When on a *hospital* elevator, my thoughts were on my husband's triple bypass operation, and not on my immediate surroundings. Everyone else got off but a young man who had been standing directly behind me. I didn't think it necessary to change positions for just one more floor. Who would have thought that such a good looking younger man would have the need to feel-up a total stranger? It happened so fast I couldn't believe it, much less, respond appropriately. My shocked shout, "I'm old enough to be your *mother!*" followed him as he quickly moved down the hall, around a corner, and out of sight.)

_____ •When walking down a sidewalk, stay close to the curb when passing large bushes, doorways, or alleys, where muggers, rapists, or stalkers can hide. Otherwise, stay away from the curb, and walk in the middle of the sidewalk.

_____ •Never place yourself in an unfamiliar area, alone, at night.

_____ •Never take a short cut down unknown streets or through alleys. The time you may save isn't worth the potential danger, worry, and stress.

_____ •If waiting anywhere alone, find a well-lit area, and stand with your back against the wall, with your cellular phone in hand.

_____ •Carry phone *coins* in your shoe or pockets, in case you lose your purse or wallet, or your cellular phone is disabled.

_____ •If eating alone in a restaurant, sit with your back against a wall or pillar, or at least sit facing the door, so you can easily see whoever or whatever is coming at you. You will feel safer, and more in control.

_____ •Watch your perimeter all the time, day or night, whether walking, biking, or just standing around. Work at extending boundaries and your peripheral vision. People watch.

_____ •Before you leave your workplace, change into comfortable shoes. Do not shop in high heels, sandals, or flip-flops. Wear flats or tennis shoes, so you can run as fast as you can, if the situation warrants it.

_____ •While shopping, if you suspect you're being followed, watch for reflections. Use large plate glass windows as rearview mirrors to check behind you.

_____ •Upon leaving any public facility, stop for a moment to assess the situation, before heading out to the parking lot or parking structure. Scan the area first.

_____ •When in public, keep your purse or briefcase on a shoulder strap, and hold it tightly under your arm—with the flap against your body—to discourage purse-snatchers.

_____ •In case of a purse snatcher or an attack, try to connect your heavy purse to the side of the mugger's face, or swing your purse or briefcase back and forth, to establish distance.

_____ •A shirt or jacket pocket is a better place to keep your wallet than a hip pocket. Disperse your money in various pockets. Some men have chosen to place their large bills in money clips in their inside jacket pockets, and are using wide rubber bands around bulkier smaller bills, situated in their back pockets. It may not be fashionable, but it's a safety issue, so who cares? The rubber band catches on the fabric, making it harder for pickpockets to extract money, without the owner's knowledge.

_____ •If the purse snatcher or pickpocket is successful, minimize the damage by carrying the bare minimum of cash and only one or two credit cards. Make sure you have copies of wallet photos, work I.D. cards, and anything else of value to you.

_____ •Know how to report stolen credit cards. Keep your credit card numbers where you can easily find them.

_____ •Never leave your purse, briefcase, or shopping bags unattended, even it they are sitting next to you. Place the bags on the floor under your feet, and keep the straps of your purse or briefcase discretely wrapped around your arms or legs, or the chair legs.

_____ •Never use an ATM at night.

_____ •Know that restrooms are considered to be the second most unsafe public place. When using a public restroom, even if it appears to be empty, check the stalls. Remain alert. Use your eyes and ears. Don't put your purse on the floor.

_____ •Sit close to an exit when at school, church, movies, et cetera.

_____ •Wherever you go, know where all of the exits are located.

_____ •If you think you're being followed, at school or while shopping, notify security, and have an agent walk you to your vehicle.

_____ •Do not do your grocery shopping at night. If it is unavoidable, park under a light as close to the store as possible, and have store personnel walk you out. They will be happy to do so (not only to keep your business, but also to avoid bad publicity).

_____ •Keep a copy of your restraining order in your pocket *and* in your purse or wallet.

_____ •Do not give any personal information on Internet chat lines.

_____ •And whatever you do, for whatever reason, don't allow yourself to be photographed in the nude, by your husband or significant other. A stalker or intruder could easily steal your private photos, and you may, at some later date, come face-to-face with your image on the Internet. Not a pretty picture.

_____ •Don't drink excessively, and never drink in restaurants or bars alone. Why needlessly set yourself up for trouble? Never, ever, leave your drink unattended. You don't want someone slipping Rohypnol or GHB ("rape drugs") into your drink. They are fast-acting, and render you unconscious. Later, you may wake up on the other side of town, or dumped along the side of the road, without any memory as to what took place, how it happened, where it happened, or who you were with. Only accept unopened cans.

_____ •Stalkers are very good at creating chance encounters. If you seem to "accidentally" bump into a person who has stalked you in the past, do not stop to chat about old times. (You'd think this would be a given, but I've met a few women who thought it was safe to do so, because of the intervening time involved. One woman even argued with me about my viewpoint, even though she admitted that the man had recently popped up at *several* public and semi-private places "coincidentally.") Get to safety. With a renewed acquaintance, your former stalker can and may reattach to you. Do not encourage any further interest. Do not toy with trouble.

VEHICLE SAFETY

_____ •Commit to improving your vehicle and driving safety.

_____ •Even if you drive an armor-reinforced car with bulletproof windows, stalkers, carjackers, robbers, and rapists all know that you are at your most vulnerable when getting in or out of your vehicle. Be aware of your surroundings before opening your door. Don't linger. Immediately shut and lock the door.

_____ •Vary your driving route to work, school, shopping, and home.

_____ •Vary your daily schedule, leaving and arriving at different times.

_____ •Use well-traveled and well-lighted streets.

_____ •Be on the alert, while driving. Do not allow the worries and stress of the day to interfere with your concentration. Put any anger, fear, anticipation, or excitement on hold. Scan your surroundings at all times. Constantly check your rearview mirror. Watch out for other cars.

_____ •If you suspect that another vehicle may be following you, try speeding up and then slowing down. If you're still not sure, make four right-hand turns, to see if it stays with you.

_____ •Drive defensively. Consider taking a Defense Driving course, or a security firm's or insurance's course in detecting and eluding surveillance.

_____ •Keep the radio volume at a level in which you can hear surrounding activity. (I can't tell you how many near misses I've seen, between cars and firetrucks. It's scary.)

_____ •When stopped at a signal, leave enough room between your car and the vehicle in front of you, for unexpected maneuvering.

_____ •Refrain from painting your vehicle an unusual color, like Purple Pizzazz or Electric Lime. Don't add fancy pinstriping, designs, or advertising. This will only make it easier to identify you. Blend in.

_____ •Do not display bumper stickers or distinctive decals that will make it easier to follow your car.

_____ •Check your brakelights. Experts tell us that stalkers may place a tiny hole in one of your taillights, or replace a bulb with a higher-intensity bulb, or simply remove a bulb, making your vehicle easier to follow from a distance. Or, he/she may instead opt to place a strip of light-reflective tape on your bumper for the same effect.

_____ •If you feel threatened, do not drive home. Go to the nearest police or sheriff's department, fire department, or college security station. Lean on your horn.

_____ •Install a car phone, or have a cell phone or a two-way radio handy at all times. If you feel that you're in danger, whenever or wherever, call and tell law enforcement that you're on your way, and to be expecting you. Invest in an automatic dialfeature. You don't want to have your hands off the wheel in such a stressful situation.

_____ •Even while driving, always keep your car doors locked. Anyone can slide into the passenger seat while you're waiting for a signal to change or are stuck in traffic. (While idling at a red light, I actually saw a woman run over and open a driver's door in the middle lane. The driver was shocked at this uninvited intrusion.)

_____ •Even when you're in waiting mode—no matter how long—keep the doors and windows shut and locked.

_____ •Childproof your door locks, to deter a stalker or burglar from popping them with a coathanger.

_____ •Equip your vehicle with an air-conditioner. It will keep you from driving with open windows.

_____ •If a pedestrian approaches your vehicle, while parked or at a stop sign, do not roll down your window.

_____ •If someone walks up to your car, asking to wash your windows, refuse. If the person fails to leave, blow your horn.

_____ •Use your horn for all kinds of emergencies. (In my early twenties, I was sitting alone, in an unlit fast-food restaurant parking lot one evening, eating a hamburger. Out of nowhere, a fight broke out between five teenagers and a much, much older man who was obviously drunk. The man called them some unflattering names, and the boys responded with testosterone urgency, by whaling the tar out of the guy. I thought the violence excessive, but was too frightened to run for help. Instead, I leaned on my horn to attract some attention. I had to honk for a good long time before people in the eating establishment got the message that there was a problem outside. The boys knocked on my window, but I wouldn't open it. Finally, as help was in the off-ing, they all ran away.)

_____ •If someone sticks a gun in your face, give up your vehicle! Your life is more important. You can always get another car. (Recently, in Long Beach, a man was killed simply for the fancy rims on his wheels.) You have insurance, don't you?

_____ •Place your purse or wallet beneath the seat. Place your packages as low down as possible, and cover them.

_____ •Drive in the middle lanes, to eliminate unwanted pedestrian problems.

_____ •Avoid congested or narrow streets, whenever possible.

_____ •Place your children in the car before you put your shopping bags in, to deter kidnapping,

_____ •Never leave your vehicle unlocked, even when just paying for gas or returning a grocery cart in the market parking lot. Carjacking is a crime of convenience, and a number of cars have been stolen with babies or toddlers strapped in their car seats. (A friend's new car was stolen as he was unloading groceries. He left the hatch up, as he took his third trip hauling multiple bags into his apartment. A stranger crawled through the hatch opening, dove into the driver's seat, and tore outta there! The owner was more embarrassed than upset. He *knew* he should have locked his car.)

_____ •Try to keep your gas tank half full. (This is hard for me.)

_____ •Always fill your gas tank during daylight hours.

_____ •If your vehicle is not equipped with an automatic gas tank opener, install a locking gas cap. Otherwise, you may find sugar or soap detergent in your tank. (This happened to my father.)

_____ •Never wash your vehicle at a Coin-Op Car Wash at night. (A friend and her husband were washing their car, not realizing how vulnerable they appeared, and were robbed at gunpoint. A robber approached while they were inconveniently stretched across the hood, soaping it, and in no position to argue. The guy made off with their jewelry and cash.)

_____ •If your vehicle is disabled, stay in the car. Turn on your emergency flashers. Use a large emergency windshield sign or a smaller visor sign, or even a hand printed sign, that says something similar to HELP! CALL 911, or CALL TOW TRUCK. Do not roll down your window. Do not accept a ride from a stranger. (You may want to keep a spiral notebook in your car, to use in case of such an emergency.)

_____ •Install a car alarm. If nothing else, it may scare away a car thief.

_____ •Consider installing a release mechanism inside your trunk. (Recently, the TV news told the story of a woman who had been accosted, beaten up, and thrown in the back of her own car. Later, the perpetrator stopped for gas, and went into the mart to pay. The woman beat on the lid of the trunk, and the attendant immediately hit the switch that raised the door, and helped her out. The carjacker/kidnapper ran away.) Installing such an inside handle/button/cable release may come in handy, on the off chance that a similar situation happens to you.

_____ •As an alternative, experts suggest, if you end up in the trunk of a car, that you kick out a tail light, and frantically wave your hand through the hole (although cramped quarters and the noise factor may hamper this advice).

_____ •Keep a First Aid kit in your vehicle.

_____ •Leave a blanket in your vehicle.

_____ •Leave an old jacket and gloves in your vehicle.

_____ •Carry a fire extinguisher in your vehicle. Keep it handy, and know how to use it. (My husband has always carried a fire extinguisher, and although he has never had occasion to use it on his own vehicles, he has put out numerous car fires for total strangers. One night, years ago, we were sitting in a drive-in theater, when the car parked behind us suddenly burst into flames. He rushed over and put out the fire, and then we waited almost a half-hour for the fire trucks to arrive. Needless to say, few people watched the movie that night.)

_____ •Make sure you buy good quality tires, ones that are known to remain stable for a number of miles, when punctured or with a slow leak. Always carry a spare tire.

_____ •Log the date when you find you have a flattened tire. One nail or piece of glass embedded in your tire can be merely an accident, but more than that, or several tires at once, point to sabotage. (I found a 10" roofing nail in my tire when it went flat. A week later, there was *another* 10" roofing nail in my tire. Does that occurrence seem coincidental to you?)

_____ •If you have a flat while driving, don't stop. Head for safety.

_____ •When being chased, don't stop. Drive in populated areas and lean on your horn.

_____ •Always wear your seatbelt. You never know when a stalker might deliberately rear-end or broadside your vehicle (both of which have happened to me).

_____ •Stalkers and carjackers are known to deliberately crash into other cars. If involved in an accident, do not leave your vehicle. Experts say to keep your doors locked, turn on your emergency flashers, and wait for the police.

_____ •Never give out your address or phone number to strangers, even with a seemingly legitimate accident. Offer only the name and number of your insurance agent.

_____ •Here in America, police cars flash red and blue lights. Experts warn that you are never get out of your car for a vehicle flashing only white lights or yellow lights.

_____ •Park under lights, close to an exit, or near attendants, if possible.

_____ •When parking, note where you are. Write it down if you are in large venues: malls, stadiums, ballparks, airports, entertainment parks, and underground or standing parking structures. You want to spend as little time as necessary looking for your vehicle. You don't want to appear vulnerable to onlookers.

_____ •Before returning to your vehicle, scan the area surrounding it for anyone who appears to be loitering. (After a hard day of shopping, a friend got in her car, and it wouldn't start. A man was sitting in a neighboring car, and asked if he could help her. She was far from the mall stores, with no cell phone to call Triple A, so she agreed that he could help. He fiddled around under the hood, and then fiddled around with the wires under the dash. He said that the wires may begin to spark, and asked her to put one foot on the brake and one foot on the accelerator, and hold a large piece of cardboard on the steering wheel, to protect her face. He then wiggled the wires some more, maneuvering under the steering wheel, to get a betterview up her dress, between her legs. He laid his head back on her ankle, and thinking that this was taking far too long, she looked down to find that the man had his hand down his pants, while looking up at hers. Still polite, she climbed out of the car, thanked him, and started toward the mall. He scampered to her hood, opened it, and reattached the distributor wire—that he had removed earlier, of course—and told her to try to start the car again. It started, and she drove on home. Her husband, a Deputy Sheriff, couldn't *believe* that his wife was so gullible and trusting. She later pointed out the man to her husband, who had a fine talk with the guy.)

_____ •Check for suspicious vehicles parked next to you. You don't want someone popping out of his van to grab you, while you are off-balance, getting into your car. Such assaults usually come from the rear of your car, as they approach you from behind. Backtrack and get security if things don't feel right.

_____ •In such a case, experts tell us to drop to the ground and roll under your vehicle, while biting, kicking, and yelling. (I'm afraid that I'm a tad too large to fit under any car.)

_____ •Always have the correct key in hand before going out to your vehicle. Don't be caught unaware, focused solely on finding your keys, as you fumble around in the bottom of your purse or slap your pockets.

_____ •Always give the backseat and passenger floorboard areas a quick visual once-over before getting in your car. Guys have been known to lie under cars, to grab women by the ankles, and pull them down. (There was even a case in Long Beach, in which a man would slice the Achille's Tendon with a straight razor, to disable women.)

_____ •The moment you enter your car, shut and lock the door. *Then* buckle your seatbelt and start the engine.

_____ •Attach a small flashlight to your keychain.

_____ •Never place your name, car license number, or anything that identifies your car, on your keychain. Anonymous is the watchword.

_____ •If you think your vehicle may have been tampered with, look for nails in the tires or cut valve stems, and check for loosened hubcaps or lug nuts. Look for evidence of spills, or the smell of gas around the gas tank, and check for brake fluid under the car. Pump your brakes. Call the police if you are the least bit suspicious.

_____ •If you have a remote door opener, make sure it opens the driver's door only. You don't want a stranger hopping in the passenger door, while you're getting in the driver's seat.

_____ •Join an auto club, in case you are ever stranded.

_____ •Do not put your name on a license plate holder (Tanya's Toyota, Merrily's Mustang), or a vanity license plate (SexySue.) Do you really need to advertise?

_____ •Do not use a window sticker or bumper sticker with your name on it.

_____ •Carry separate weapons in your vehicle: pepper spray, heavy-duty aluminum flashlight, hammer, whatever works well for you. (Make sure you carry nothing illegal). Know exactly where each is located. Make sure they are easy to retrieve.

_____•Never pick up hitchhikers or strangers, even if they appear to be stranded. Call 911, or a tow truck, for them.

_____ •Keep your vehicle keys separate from your house keys.

_____ •Do not magnetize a spare key hide-a-box anywhere outside your vehicle.

_____ •Consider buying a locking device for your steering wheel, such as the Club. It may deter a crime of convenience. (One day, as I pulled into a parking space, a man walked up to the door of the car that was parked next to me. I noticed that he seemed to be having some trouble with his key, as it took him a little longer to get into the car. As he was backing out, a woman came up, pushing her cart of groceries, and started screaming, "He's stealing my car! That's my car!" She could have used a secondary locking device.)

_____ •Some experts suggest that you back your vehicle into the driveway for a fast getaway (especially if family violence is an issue).

_____ •Install an electric garage door opener, that automatically lights up when the door opens, and stays lit for a good length of time. (The inconvenience and money I spent on this item was well worth the effort.)

_____ •Make sure the area surrounding your garage is well lighted.

_____ •If your garage is attached to your house, once inside, close the garage door immediately, and look around before unlocking and opening your doors.

_____ •Consider installing closet door mirrors on both inside garage walls—adjacent to the large garage door—to reflect the presence of an intruder who my have crouched down behind your vehicle and followed you inside. Check the mirrors before unlocking your door and exiting your car. (One gorgeous woman's story was on the TV news, when she was beaten and left for dead, in her garage. Months later, she now slowly hobbles around with long leg-braces and a walker, she has a distinct speech impediment, and brain damage that left her without a memory of her first 37 years of life.)

_____ •Always lock your vehicle at night, even if it's in your garage.

_____ •Always lock your garage.

_____ •If you live in an apartment building, make sure that your assigned parking space never displays your name or your apartment number.

_____ •Always park in lighted areas, preferably well-lit and secured parking lots.

_____ •Avoid parking next to vans and other large vehicles, whenever possible.

_____ •Even during daylight hours, if you feel apprehensive, ask mall security or a store manager to walk you out to your car.

_____ •Upon approaching your vehicle, if you find a note taped to the window, or placed under your windshield wipers, leave it be. Do not open it. Get to safety, and find security or call the police. Your stalker could still be lurking close by, and you may need a witness, as well as an official to handle the evidence.

_____ •Have nothing in your vehicle that displays your address or telephone number or place of work. (Recently, many cars in my area have been broken into, for purposes of identity theft alone. Hijacking is not the purpose, nor are those responsible trying to steal the contents in the cars. All these thieves want is personal information, so that they can assume someone's identity: bank accounts, credit card numbers, social security number, addresses, work site, and so on).

_____ •Keep either a still or video camera in your vehicle, to document that your stalker is following you. Use a camera that automatically stamps the date and time on the photo. Otherwise, develop the film immediately, and place the date of the incident on the back. (I've never had an occasion to use one myself, but I've heard of others doing so. A case was aired on *America's Most Wanted* TV show, in which a woman was able to take a clear photograph of the driver in his car, and it was used in court to identify him). Be prepared.

_____ •When you purchase a new vehicle, remember that safety comes before image. Do not buy a convertible, as you'll always feel like a sitting duck in a shooting gallery. Even if you always keep the top up, you must still invest in a roll bar. If you don't have children, buy a two-door car. Make sure it has power doors and windows, and air-conditioning. You don't need a moon roof, as that offers an intruder one more way to enter your car. Understand that vehicles sitting higher off the ground—vans, pickup trucks, and SUVs—enable you to scan a much larger area, while at the same time, prohibiting those passengers in lower vehicles from seeing into your car. Having more horsepower is a must for faster acceleration. Check out your brand's safety record before signing on the dotted line. Look for the best standard safety features in the class you choose. Some vehicles are shown to fall apart in a 5-mph crash, requiring considerable time in a body shop. Could you survive a crash in it? Others are top-heavy, having serious rollover problems. Is it reliable? Can it stop on a dime? Can it make an easy U-turn, or is it too large and cumbersome to make a three-point turn? Are maintenance costs reasonable? What kind of gas mileage does it get? Consider, too, if it is a model that gets targeted by professional burglars—SUVs and sports cars—for its airbags, seats, and parts. Or is it a model that is frequently stolen, for its high resale value on the black market? (I had three cars stolen in one year! Not fun.) Consider a generic model, in a neutral color. (No one could believe—with my bombastic personality and affinity for color—that I bought a *white* car.) Looks and popularity aren't everything. Make an informed decision.

_____ •Experts suggest—especially when buying a car—that you do not give up your Social Security number or mother's maiden name until you are ready to buy. Credit applications that accompany a sale are not at risk. However, if you decide *not* to buy, take your application and credit report with you, and destroy them. (California's Taskforce for Regional Auto-theft Prevention—TRAP—is being overrun with identity theft cases, due to the sharp rise in the number of car dealership employees using credit applications to illegally secure auto loans. It is not a controlled situation.)

_____ •Consider buying your new car through a trust.

_____ •Keep your vehicle in good operating condition. Locate a reliable mechanic or dealer for service and repairs, and then give him/her all your repeat business. Follow the manufacturer's recommended maintenance schedule.

_____ •Keep enough cash on hand, or a low balance on a specific credit card, to afford emergency car repairs, as needed.

_____ •Consider joining LoJack, a system for locating and recovering stolen cars. Their advertising states that a car is stolen every 25.7 seconds, and that LoJack has a 90 percent recovery rate.

_____ •Always keep a pen and paper handy, so you can jot down license plate numbers or descriptions of vehicles. (While traveling down the freeway, five teenagers in the car in front of me were acting quite suspiciously. When I saw a gun being passed from the front seat to the back, it became clear to me that they had been involved in a robbery. I immediately wrote down the license and car description, the number of passengers, and so forth. I followed them until they took an off ramp. I stopped at the next freeway emergency phone, and called in the information. Shortly thereafter, a police car pulled up right behind me, and I was questioned further by an officer, who would repeat the information over his mike. Since I was on my way to a mystery writers group meeting, I had an exciting tale to tell.)

_____ •Keep a copy of your restraining order and your flyer in your vehicle.

WORK SAFETY

_____ •Be more mindful of job safety, as you are more accessible at your place of employment than anywhere else. Commit to improving your own security at work. (Do you know: Are employee records and information truly private? How are duplicate keys to offices, desks, and file cabinets handled? How easy is it for anyone to get into your computer? If you work in a small office, how is the trash handled?)

_____ •Does the company stress violence prevention? If harassed by a co-worker, what are your company's procedures for in-house improper behavior or threats? Would that person be fired, or would *you* be fired if lower on the totem pole, or would it simply be suggested that he/she seek private outside psychological services, or emphatically ordered to enroll in on-site therapy? Is there a procedure already set in place?

_____ •Ask about proper procedures concerning workplace violence and protection. Many victims are harassed via the work telephone. Realize that close to half of all stalkers show up at the work site of their victims. (As a restaurant hostess, I was harassed on the phone to such a degree, that patrons couldn't call in their reservations. Since I refused to speak to my caller on the phone, he came in person. It was difficult to do my job, when he sat there staring at me.)

_____ •Inform the appropriate supervisor and/or boss of your situation. Give them each a flyer. (A friend was considered so indispensable at her place of business, that the boss took unusual measures. He had the front of the building—which was simply one humongus plate glass window—painted with a special paint, so that those inside could see out, but those outside couldn't see in; like a one-way mirror. And he hired a bodyguard for her, for the full eight hours she was at work each day. She and the bodyguard ate lunch together in various restaurants, and he accompanied her wherever she went, that was work-related. Can you *imagine*?)

_____ •Ask about flexible and/or alternative work hours.

_____ •Inform your work security detail, and give them a copy of your restraining order, as well as a flyer. If you work in a large office building, introduce yourself to the security detail. Know their names. Be friendly and chat with them, as you come and go. (At two university sites, because I left after ten at night, security personnel would always walk me out to my car. And I've never had a problem. However, three young women gang members, who didn't like the grades they were receiving, accosted a professor friend in the university elevator. Apparently, the trio had not yet made the emotional leap from the ghetto. The professor was petrified. Luckily for her, when the doors opened, a security man just happened to be walking by, and she called out to him to escort her to her car. She later quit because of this incident.)

_____ •Establish a plan for a course of action, if no official guidelines or policies are in place. Take reasonable precautions.

_____ •Inform your coworkers of your situation. Give them each one of your flyers. (You may lose some friends this way, as some won't want to be standing around you, if or when something hits the fan. Take solace in the fact that, at least, you warned them.)

_____ •To educate your coworkers, you may want to have a stalking expert or a victim advocate give a presentation at one of your worksite meetings, to answer questions and hand out informational brochures.

_____ •If your stalker is seen on the premises, the police should be called immediately.

_____ •Make sure that only a couple of well-trusted individuals (who can't be duped!) have your home phone number, and can be trusted not to give it, or your personal information, to anyone for any reason.

_____ •Make sure that your address and phone numbers aren't included in a company directory. (When I taught in a public school, everyone who was faculty or staff for the entire school district was included in the yearly directory. One year, some robbers got a hold of it, and had themselves a fine time, looting the houses of teachers. Knowing the time the schools let out, the robbers backed up moving vans in the early morning, taking their time, while stealing every item in the houses—up to, and including, the toilet paper rolls. One teacher became unstrung, because the robbers even took her pet bird.) Be advised.

_____ •Have coworkers monitor the phones for you.

_____ •Have someone else record the message on your voice mail. (Some stalkers have been known to tie up the phone lines by repeatedly calling, just to hear their victims' voice.)

_____ •Have coworkers monitor any personal mail for you.

_____ •Ensure that strangers don't have access to your work area. The receptionist, secretary, or front office staff should never allow those without authorization to have contact with you. Reinforce the message whenever new employees are hired.

_____ •Position your desk to face the door. Try to have a wall behind you. You will feel more relaxed when you can see who is entering the room.

_____ •If your stalker knows where your office space is located, ask to be moved to another site that is more secure—a different room, store, or branch. (One man drove his truck through the wall of the office of his intended victim, smashing into her desk. Luckily, a few days prior, she had switched to an office upstairs.)

_____ •Remove your nameplate from your door and desk.

_____ •Insist that your home address and personal telephone or cell phone numbers are not printed on your business cards. Do not display them on your desk. Hand out cards only as needed.

_____ •Do not display framed family photos at work. Do not even leave a "World's Best Mom/Dad" coffee mug on your desk. Don't give away any clues of your home situation. Share your family stories with only a trusted few.

_____ •Do not keep any personal information about you or your family on, or in, your desk, computer, or workspace. Know who has access to your computer.

_____ •If it is imperative that you keep some personal phone numbers in your Rolodex, use a code, nicknames, or initials, to keep your family and friends private.

_____ •Do not leave your work calendar out on top of your desk, where any-one can easily see your schedule. When a stalker knows your future plans, he/she can easily show up at the site of your destination.

_____ •File your important papers in a file cabinet that locks. Make sure that you are the only person with a key.

_____ •Do not let your name or photo be displayed on walls, bulletin boards, or displaycases, where the general public can easily see them.

_____ •Know multiple ways out of your work site.

_____ •Scope out some suitable hiding places, just in case.

_____ •Locate the fire alarm buttons or switches, to use in an emergency situation.

_____ •Vary your lunchtime, and eating establishments, if possible. Go with a group, or eat on-site.

_____ •Do not arrive at work before your colleagues.

_____ •Never stay late at work, after your coworkers have left.

_____ •Walk out to the parking area in a group, or have a security member walk you to your car.

_____ •Vary your driving route to and from your place of work.

_____ •Park in a well-lit garage, or in an outdoor area that is secured, or observable.

_____ •Do not use a parking slot that displays your name.

_____ •Vary your parking spots on a daily basis.

_____ •When registering for business meetings, conferences, or conventions, sign only your name; write the address and phone number of your company or lawyer or mail box, without comment. Do not write down your personal home information. Anyone who fills out a sign-in sheet is privy to all the data written above. (As a student teacher supervisor, I visit many school sites each week. Some of the schools require visitors to write their addresses and phone numbers on the Visitor's Sheet, in addition to surrendering their car keys. The Visitor's sheet is left out for anyone to view. Not good.)

_____ •In California, employers can get restraining orders against stalkers, and a number of nationally-known companies have done so, to protect their employees. Check to see if your state and/or company supports this procedure.

_____ •Change jobs, if imperative. (It's not *fair*, but this is a safety consideration.) However, know upfront, that if you stay in the same type of profession, you can easily be traced—confidentiality being next to nil—unless you also change your name. Consider, too, whether your new boss will want to put up with a potential stalking problem. After all, he/she has no prior investment in you (neither a working relationship nor a friendship history). Workplace stalking situations are often reported in the media, so the general public is well aware that the second most likely target is anyone who is perceived to be interfering with access to the victim. Intervention increases the risk of violence. Seemingly, more third party victims are maimed and killed than the actual targets. (The U.S. Postal Service had 38 employees murdered in a seven-year span, giving rise to the phrase, "going postal.") When a stalker shows up at a victim's work site, the resulting disruptions are seen to have devastating effects on employee morale, as well as productivity, whether or not there is violence. And, coupled with the knowledge that homicide is now the leading cause of death for women in the workplace, it is no wonder that employers think carefully about applicants with a potential problem. So, unfortunately, instead of being seen as a great employee and an asset to the organization, you might just represent unwanted and unneeded future trouble: a liability; a risk factor. (Some victims have been *fired*, simply because they are being stalked.) The employer must weigh the safety of a new, unknown employee against that of the rest of the old, known workforce. It is not an easy decision to make, from a business standpoint or a moral point of view, especially given the serious legal questions involved. Understand from the get-go that you may be giving up physical, emotional, and social support from former coworkers, that will be entirely lacking in your new place of employment.

_____ •If you work out of your home, make sure that you use a private mail box address on all of your stationary, envelopes, business cards, and advertising. (I spent six hundred dollars on new stationary and envelopes alone, before I realized my mistake. Oh, woe!)

TRAVEL SAFETY

_____ •Commit to improving your travel safety measures. Good preparation is paramount for travel safety and security.

_____ •Let only family and close friends know your destination plans and tentative schedule. Call and let them know when things change.

_____ •Whether you're a celebrity, a local figure, or an unknown, never allow your flight plan, schedule, or hotel information to be published. Don't publicly announce your visit.

_____ •When traveling in an unfamiliar city or country, do your homework. Call ahead to find out about the streets, neighborhoods, and areas to avoid.

_____ •If you are renting a vehicle, make sure that you know how to operate that particular make and model before leaving the premises. (Before seatbelts were mandatory, I flew into Utah and rented a car. The seatbelts automatically enclosed me, and I about had a stroke: I thought I was being attacked, and screamed and fought with the seatbelt until my cooler head prevailed.)

_____ •Make sure that you have specific directions to your destination before driving. As an AAA member, you can get free maps easily. And although most rental car establishments will be happy to help you with directions, if you don't want anyone else to know your itinerary, obtain a computerized printout of your complete trip through various websites: **www.mapquest.com; www.expedia.com; www.vicinity.com/geocities/driving.html,** and the like. Besides giving you step-by-step directions, the printout will tell you the exact mileage from place to place, as well as the estimated time involved, places of interest, places to eat, and so forth.

_____ •Consider using chain gas station or restaurant restrooms, instead of rest stops, whenever possible.

_____ •When traveling out of town, hide your money. Wear a money belt, an ankle/arm wallet, or a small pouch that hangs inconspicuously from your neck under your clothes; use lingerie items with hidden pockets, zippered sock compartments, or simply pin some bills to the inside of your trousers, vest, or skirt. Use discretion. (I gave my father a money belt when he moved to New Orleans, but he was so delighted with the gift, he continually showed it to total strangers, in his hotel elevator, and taxicabs. Not good.) Check catalogs for specialty items: 4"x4" hidden zippered wallets to hang from your neck that can carry cash, keys, and credit cards; cell phone cases that have built-in wallets; zippered socks, and so on.

_____ •Take photocopies of important documents: driver's license, passport, traveler's checks, and credit card numbers. Leave copies at home, keep copies at work, and take copies with you. (My niece lost her passport *twice* in Australia—a costly and time consuming experience—and those copies saved her bacon.)

_____ •Make sure you have a credit card to use for emergencies (not purchases) in case you lose your passport.

_____ •Wear a medical alert ID bracelet, if you have a major medical condition.

_____ •Carry a medical alert ID card, listing your blood type, any current medical conditions you may have, as well as the medications you are taking. Include any food allergies (such as shellfish, chocolate, peanuts, or sulfites used as preservatives), drink (alcohol, or lactose intolerance) or environmental allergies (airborne substances, animal allergies, chemicals); medications to which you have reactions (penicillin, antibiotics), sensitivities (perfume, aftershave, latex, smoke), and susceptibility to insect bites (mosquitoes, biting flies, chiggers, fleas, ticks, and some spiders), in addition to allergic reactions to insect stings (bees, wasps, hornets, yellow jackets, Fire Ants, or scorpions). Include recent vaccinations.

_____ •Make sure you carry your medications with you in your carry-on bags, in their original prescription containers. Luggage is often lost. (My sister-in-law traveled to China. While there, she purchased numerous Christmas gifts for her large family, placing them in two large brand new suitcases for the return trip. They were stolen, after having been checked in, at the airport.)

_____ •Consider packing a flashlight, with extra batteries. (I've been registered in two hotels during major power outages, where a flashlight would have been worth its weight in gold. Being on the 12th floor, with no elevators in operation, and no lights in the stairwells, is unnerving.)

_____ •If you plan to do any reading whatsoever, you may want to pack a 100 watt lightbulb, since most hotels use soft or low lighting.

_____ •Do not carry pepper spray or a mini-baton on airplanes.

_____ •After a flight, do not join the masses around the baggage carousels. Stand back and wait to gather your suitcases until the crowd has thinned. You can be an easy target in an anonymous crowd.

_____ •Make the effort to get reservations before you arrive.

_____ •When registering, park close to the front of the hotel.

_____ •Make sure you hand your vehicle keys to an attendant who is wearing the hotel uniform or insignia. Give him/her only your car key.

_____ •Time your arrival at the registration desk with a group of people, so as not to call attention to the fact that you are alone.

_____ •If you have a choice, do not stay on the first or second floors (easy access for an intruder), or above the twelfth floor (fire equipment reaches no higher in most cities).

_____ •Request a room that doesn't share a balcony.

_____ •Make sure the check-in counter clerk doesn't compromise your safety by saying your name, or room number, aloud. If people are standing within hearing distance, quietly request another room on another floor.

_____ •Consider checking in under a pseudonym.

_____ •Place your valuables in a safe deposit box at the front desk, whether or not there is a private wall safe in your room. An intruder can certainly threaten you, convincing you to open the safe yourself.

_____ •Experts advise that you have a hotel employee check your room, ensuring that it is empty, before you enter. Check all rooms, the closet, the shower stall, and under the beds.

_____ •Never directly open the door when it is knocked upon. Ask for a name and the reason for the interruption. When you request a delivery, ask at the time of the order, for the name of the delivery person. If the knocker can't give you the proper name, do not open the door. Call security.

_____ •Be aware of anyone loitering around in the hallways, or those who get off the elevator with you. Stand back, and let them proceed first. (My brother-in-law left a casino floor with thirty thousand dollars in winnings, rode up the elevator, and was followed directly into his room. When he awoke, he was minus his cash.)

_____ •Acquaint yourself with the fire exits upon arrival. If a fire alarm sounds, leave immediately, and get down to the ground floor. (In one hotel where my husband stayed, the guests wouldn't leave because they couldn't *smell* fire, and didn't want to be inconvenienced. In another, I observed that even though fire personnel and equipment were all over the place, with smoke and fire obvious, and the overhead sprinklers had kicked on, the guests didn't want to leave the gaming tables. Finally, the staff picked up the tables and moved them out to the patio around the pool, where the playing continued. In yet a third hotel, my husband and I were enjoying an early lunch, having no idea that a wing of the huge complex was on fire. No managers or loud speakers announced that fact. Finally, when some gurneys were wheeled past the restaurant's open doors, we realized that something was definitely wrong.) Stay alert to changes in atmosphere and crowd patterns.

_____ •To preserve your privacy, watch what you say on the phone, as generally, all calls go through the hotel switchboard, where there may be eavesdroppers.

_____ •When abroad, be inconspicuous. Don't advertise your nationality by wearing red, white, and blue or clothes or patches displaying the Stars and Stripes. Don't call attention to yourself with T-shirt slogans in English (especially those with a political bent, or even the slightest bit suggestive or pornographic, or those with in-your-face graphics). Don't display religious items, or corporate logos. Don't make it easy for others to target you as an American or to take offense. Blend in.

_____ •Know the culture in which you'll be traveling. Be aware of local customs and taboos. You don't want to unwittingly insult the host country. Misunderstandings can easily take place.

_____ •Always travel in pairs or in a group.

_____ •Avoid tourist traps and nightclubs, if you are alone.

_____ •Be wary of swarms of children. They may try to distract you so others can pick your pockets.

_____ •If waiting for a taxi, bus, or subway, stand back from the curb, and near a group of people.

_____ •Glance around to see if there is anyone who appears more interested in the people than the transportation. You may be looking at a pickpocket, purse snatcher, or mugger.

_____ •Sit as close to the bus driver as possible, so as to solicit information if you aren't familiar with the area, as well as to inform him/her of any potential trouble. The driver can call for help. (When my husband was visiting Seattle for the Goodwill Games in 1990, he observed a theft taking place in the back of the late-night bus. Four Russians visitors— who had been heavily drinking, and did not have their wits about them—were being relieved of their wallets by seven local gang members. He was able to inform the bus driver.)

_____ •Do not sit next to anyone in a bus, train, or on the subway that makes you uncomfortable. Change seats.

_____ •If you start to get off the bus or subway, and see or feel signs of trouble (a dark area that should be brightly lit, suspicious acting people), don't get off.

_____ •You need not take the first taxi in line. Simply step back and let another individual or group go ahead of you. (A cab driver fight ensued in Cancun, when four of us elected to take a different cab. It was a scary experience. Many other taxis chased our cab, yelling obscenities, while trying to block it. We should have been more discrete about choosing another ride—feigning a phone call, or waiting for a latecomer, or some such excuse.)

_____ •If your taxi driver appears to be acting strangely, or driving in an erratic and/or unsafe manner, pay the driver, get out, and hail another cab. (I had a wild taxi ride in New York that I'll never forget! The driver was aiming his cab at pedestrians in the street while stomping on the gas, and laughing maniacally when they barely made it back to the curb in time. His reasoning was that those people had no business in "his" street.)

_____ •Don't share a taxi with a stranger.

_____ •Don't let your curiosity get in the way of good judgment. If a confrontation looks like its brewing between a couple of people, walk away. When you see a mob forming (a sporting event riot, an impromptu gang gathering, a civil disturbance, a rally, a political protest march or demonstration) quickly remove yourself from the area. You don't need to be in the thick of things. Read about it later in the newspaper, or watch the TV news in the safety of your hotel room.

_____ •Keep focused on your safety and security when out and about. Don't distract yourself with business matters, personal concerns and worries, or random thoughts. Be vigilant. Don't let your guard down, upon returning to your home city.

PHYSICAL HEALTH

_____ •You are responsible for your own physical health. It is easy to ignore or minimize your bodily needs, when safety is the dominant issue. Commit to taking care of yourself physically.

_____ •Understand that your heightened and sustained stress levels can affect the rest of your life. Be aware that medical problems can be attributed to abuse, stalking, assault, or rape trauma: from headaches, stomachaches, backaches, rashes, colds and the flu, to more serious conditions of ulcers, diabetes, hypertension, and heart problems.

_____ •Stalking is a marathon event, played out over a good length of time. Know that the prolonged stress of always being on the alert and on the defensive, can adversely impact your immune system, leaving you with a very low resistance to illness and disease. You may become plagued with headaches, the flu, or infections. You may notice that your colds linger, bruises take longer to fade, and cuts heal more slowly. Endurance is key. You need to be in top form to deal with the stress of a stalking situation. Take care of your bodily needs.

_____ •Understand that stress increases your nutritional needs. Take vitamins and minerals for your all-around health (A, B, C, D, E, Calcium, Iron, Magnesium, Potassium, and zinc). If this seems like too much to handle at first, take at least one good multivitamin/multimineral dietary supplement daily, as a start. You need all the help you can get.

_____ •While under a stalking siege, there is often a marked increase or decrease in food intake. (At first, I lost so much weight, I looked like a skeleton with my ribs sticking out. It's easy to let your interest in food slide. After finally regaining my ideal weight, however, I then packed on another sixty pounds.)

_____ •As the saying goes: Stressed spelled backwards is desserts. Many people eat sweets when under stress, existing on a diet of donuts, rolls, candy bars and caffeinated sodas to achieve an added adrenaline boost. (This was my menu for years!) Realize that the boost lasts less than an hour, before your blood sugar plummets, and you start the cycle again. Fight that temptation. Eat three solid meals, or five smaller meals, daily.

Juice or Smoothies are better than sodas. Make food choices your body can *live* with, that boost your physical health with fortifying, immunity-boosting, nutritional powers.

_____ •A stalker appears to be a vampire, constantly sucking away your energy. The perpetual stress of fear, shock, anger, and helplessness will eventually reach their limit, and you'll be plunged into a state of fatigue. Consciously keep up your endurance level by snacking on raisins, trailmix, bran muffins, carrot sticks, fruit, or juices, and other healthy alternatives. (I know, I know. If it practically takes an act of Congress to get you to eat a vegetable or a piece of fruit, if you worry when your stash of junk food is running low, if you're a sugar freak like I am, this tip is hard to swallow. It's easier if you plan ahead and have a supply of healthy munchies available at your fingertips.) You can't afford to let your physical self deteriorate. Why give your stalker yet *another* advantage?

_____ •Remember to breathe. We all naturally hold our breath when surprised or dumbfounded. (All these years later, my husband reminds me to breath every now and then, when I've received bad news, or whatever.)

_____ •Breathe deeply. Shallow breathing appears during times of fear, anger, and stress. Both doctors and fitness experts say that such rapid inhalations pump air in and out of your throat, without getting into your lungs (making you easily winded and fatigued). Consciously slow your breath. Just a slight change in your breathing can be enough to cause a shift in your well-being. Steady deep breathing calms your mind (allowing you to think clearly), and relaxes your muscles. Let oxygen restore your cells, as well as your focus. It is often said that fresh air not only brings about fresh ideas, but a fresh point of view.

_____ •If you're anxious, nervous, or stressed out, don't just sit there agitating. Do something *physical* as a release. It's far better to clean the house, weed the garden, jump rope, play hop scotch or hula hoop, than to simply stew and scramble your brain. Even pacing is better than doing nothing at all.

_____ •Research shows that physical exercise provides the greatest health benefit. Standard fitness guidelines recommend a minimum thirty minutes of moderately vigorous exercise three times a week. Be firm in your commitment to become moderately fit. Tolerate your discomfort. (After all, if you can deal with the continual trauma of a stalking experience, you can deal with a little physical discomfort *of your own choosing*, in your effort to thwart a stalker or an attacker). Do it for yourself, through sheer force of will. Be patient and persistent, and your discomfort will soon go by the wayside. Like the ads say, just do it. No excuses. No whining.

_____ •Setting up and following a physical fitness program (walking, yoga, tai-chi, self-defense class, martial arts, weight training, aerobics, whatever), demonstrates that you are taking charge of your life, and are acting on your own behalf. Be realistic. Make your pace reasonable, steady, and purposeful. Do not overdo. Your new discipline and self-control will bring about a sense of accomplishment that will keep you focused and moving in the right direction. Consistency counts. Focus on experiencing *small*, achievable, physical goals, and improve your self-esteem.

_____ •When feeling low or lethargic, experts determine that physical exercise will mobilize your energy, and further, that it is as effective as medication for the blahs, a bad mood, or depression. It is said that walking for only five minutes a day can reduce anxiety and lift your spirits. Know that you will survive times of turbulence and stress much better if you regularly exercise.

_____ •In addition, exercise is a great way to burn off your irritability, anger, or rage (which is certainly better than displacing it, by heaping it on your family members or coworkers.) Discharge all that negative energy through cleaning, building, dancing, or playing. *Doing* something is key to overcoming solitary moping.

_____ •Be mindful of the fact that stalking, assault, and rape victims, may be in danger of overdoing the consumption of alcohol. Watch your intake. You don't want yet another problem.

_____ •Drug addiction (marijuana, heroin, cocaine, et cetera) may also develop in an attempt to deal with the aftereffects of stalking or rape.

_____ •Monitor your sleep patterns. Your night habits may change drastically. Determine if it takes longer to go to sleep. You may become more sensitive to noise, and awaken frequently. Abnormal restlessness and bouts of insomnia are common. (For over 40 years now, it has been extremely hard for me to fall asleep, and then, when it finally happens, with every minor bump or the slightest thump I hear, I'm wide awake with the adrenaline flowing. I then proceed to roam through the house in the dark. I rarely have a solid night's sleep.)

_____ •Experts agree that certain scents—such as chamomile, vanilla, and sandalwood—have a sedative effect. You might consider: sniffing essential oil straight from the bottle or a cotton ball, using a commercial electric diffuser or an aroma lamp, spraying the scent from a misting bottle, bathing in it, using a scented candle, or sleeping with a lavender sachet under your pillow.

_____ •It is said that if you're craving caffeine, you're probably having too little sleep or poor-quality sleep.

_____ •Be careful of self-medicating, and taking too many tranquilizers. You don't want to become addicted.

_____ •Be wary of taking too many over-the-counter sedatives. Consider the fact that sleep-producing drugs build up a tolerance in a short period of time, becoming ineffective, so you need to take larger doses for the same effect. In addition, sleeping pills interfere with your REM sleep. Don't become dependent upon them. Also, consider the fact that your alertness will be curtailed. You may not even *hear* an intruder, due to the sleeping drugs you are taking.

_____ •Check with your doctor concerning the best sleep dietary supplements (niacin, melatonin, valerian, St. John's wort, catnip, hops, et cetera). Understand the potentially harmful side effects of mixing your prescription medicines with herbal remedies. And, too, know that some herbs are therapeutic at low dosages, but toxic at higher dosages. Check it out. If unsure, your best course of action may simply be bananas and warm milk, or a slice of turkey, or a small sandwich. (A bowl of cereal helps me to fall asleep.)

_____ •Implement whatever relaxation measures work for you, prior to bedtime (Chamomile tea, soft music, a bubble bath, candles, fountains, chimes, chants, nature sounds, no late night TV news, reading spiritual material, the scent of Jasmine, and so forth).

_____ •Try to take naps, or catnaps, whenever possible.

_____ •Do not neglect your personal appearance (clean body, brushed teeth, shaved or appropriate make-up, hair combed, presentable clothes). The extra effort that goes into your appearance helps you feel good about yourself. Studies show that the less you care for your body, the worse you feel about yourself. Make good grooming a daily priority.

_____ •Pay attention to your body sensations. Do not discount what it is trying to say.

_____ •Because you become hypervigilant—on constant alert—your muscles will tense, your adrenaline will be constantly at work, and your heart will race. Consider massages. (I was so out of touch with my body, I didn't know *what* it needed. Nor could I relax. Ever. My body became as stiff as a board, and so tense that it took a year of massages before I was able to unbend. Later, I had a Pavlovian response, in which I would fall asleep as soon as I lay down on the massage table. Now *that's* progress!)

_____ •Your physiological reactions (involuntary jumping in response to unexpected noise or movement, shaking, sweating, and nausea), may become extensive and lasting. Monitor your reactions.

_____ •Statistics show that a woman is raped every minute in the USA, and that one out of every three women will be raped in their lifetime. As such, every woman is at risk. If assaulted or raped outside your home, immediately get to the hospital. Research shows that the majority of rapes happen in the victim's own home. In that event, call 911. In either case, the police or an ambulance will transport you to the closest hospital that has a Sexual Assault Response Team—SART—on site. (Counties differ in the number of SARTs that are available. For instance, there are 10 designated hospitals in Los Angeles County, whereas there is only one in Orange County: the Anaheim Memorial Medical Center.) Determine to be checked out by local health professionals immediately. You may have suffered a far greater trauma than is readily apparent, especially if you are in an unclear and disbelieving, state of shock. This is no time to feel ashamed or guilty. Get the proper services, whether you *think* you need them or not. Confused and emotionally overwrought, you'll be in no position to judge your physical condition, and you won't be making the best of decisions. (A friend thought she was fine, and it turned out later that she had a broken arm; I thought I was fine, and ended up staying in the hospital for two weeks.)

_____ •Understand that when sex is nonconsensual, there are certain physiological differences that are apparent to doctors (signs of forced entry, lacerations around the labia, tears in the vaginal wall, traces of sperm and DNA, and so on).

_____ •After a rape, your whole body is considered to be a crime scene, from which evidence can be recovered. Do not clean yourself up. Do not take a shower or a bath, or douche, as you may wash away some of the evidence. Do not even go to the bathroom, as you may be destroying other proof. Do not change your clothes, as the perpetrator's blood, saliva, hair, or semen may be on them. (Don't worry, you will be given a clothing kit of some sort—usually including clean sweats and rubber flip-flops to wear—with added amenities.) Do not straighten up the area, as the attack scene needs to be photographed.

_____ •You will be checked by a sexual assault examiner, who will treat you with understanding and compassion. Cooperate with the examiner, as she/he must collect the evidence in a timely and correct manner. The examiner must follow a step-by-step procedure. Know that any variation from the standards required to collect the forensic evidentiary material might prevent their admissibility in court, which could prevent the prosecution of the person responsible for your rape. So be cooperative. It's in your best interests.

_____ •First, X-rays are taken to find any breaks and fractures, scans are used to check for soft tissue damage, and a forensic photographer will document any cuts, bruises, abrasions, contusions, and imprints that are visible.

_____ •The rape kit seal is broken, to reveal sanitized white envelopes, which designate ten steps to be completed for evidence collection: (1) Debris evidence, where you will be asked to stand on paper as you carefully disrobe, so that anything that falls off the clothing—dirt, sand, fibers, and so forth—will be collected; (2) Dried Secretions evidence, in which your body will be scanned with a Wood's lamp (similar to a blacklight). It's a long-wave ultraviolet light, that shows semen stains, and other positive substance samples and materials, that can't be seen with the naked eye; (3) External Genital Examination evidence to retrieve samples from the exterior vaginal area; (4) Pubic Combings evidence, to find the rapist's hairs, fibers, and so on; (5) Oral Samples; (6) Rectal Samples; (7) Internal Vaginal Samples; (8) Vaginal Lavage, in which sterile water rinse is used for residual DNA or semen; (9) Urine Sample; and (10), a Reference Blood Sample is taken. All of the evidence will be carefully catalogued, placed in the packets, signed, dated, and sealed, to maintain the chain of custody, in order to be of use in a court of law. It will be handed over to the attending law enforcement officer, to be taken to each individual station, for the booking of evidence.

_____ •In addition, you will be checked and monitored for pregnancy, signs of infection, and—over a period of time—for sexually transmitted diseases, such as Herpes, Gonorrhea, AIDS, and the like, as well as other physical problems, and post-traumatic stress.

_____ •The results constitute a police problem, without question. A medical report will provide powerful evidence, even if there is no *serious* physical injury involved. Just think of it as one more indignity you have to endure, to get justice.

_____ •Keep in mind that body fat is a form of self-protection; that overweight people often have fears buried deep within themselves.

_____ •Practice self-acceptance and self-compassion. Be good to yourself.

MENTAL HEALTH

_____ •You are responsible for your own mental health. Commit to taking care of yourself mentally. Get your brain in gear by taking charge. This is not the time to be wishy-washy about anything. This is not the time to sit around and let *others* do your thinking for you. Resolve to forge your own way through problems and obstacles. You must stay totally involved, knowledgeable, and informed.

_____ •What you do today is important, because you are exchanging a day of your life for it. Know that your attention to self-protection may *save* you many more days in the future.

_____ •Understand that neither intellect, formal education, family background, life experience, age, nor competence, guarantee that you'll make the best dating choices or spousal selection. After all, you'll have made such decisions based upon misleading and incomplete information. Experts agree that a romantic misstep doesn't make you "at fault" for the predicament you may find yourself in.

_____ •Make mental awareness a part of your daily life. Consciously confront the mental obstacles in your path of self-safety and self-care. True, it is easy for you to feel constantly outraged and furious. Justifiably so. Know, however, that constantly resenting your stalker, abuser, or intruder only allows him/her to live rent-free in your head.

_____ •Your mind will continually leap from one thing to the next, in a state of dizzy distraction, if you allow it. You need to stop the mindless, out-of-control merry-go-round that tilts and whirls in your head, endlessly *re*stoking your anger, and wasting your time. Take control. Rein in those random thoughts and mental temper tantrums. Get your mindset off the unfairness and injustice of it all, and focus on *surviving*. Think, concentrate. Pull your awareness back each time it wonders, and eventually, you will release the obsessive thoughts that swirl around in your brain. Don't let this devastating experience ruin the rest of your life.

_____ •Step off the hamster wheel by saying affirmations. Affirmations—positive words, phrases, meaningful poems, or prayers—can help you to keep your attention focused and in the present. ("My good flows to me now.") They are useful tools for breaking persistent and stressful thought cycles. (If you're in the midst of a dangerous situation, such as a rape, your mantra would be, "I will survive this. I will survive!")

_____ •Understand that you must help yourself first, before anyone else can. Watch out for negative thoughts, and substitute them with positive words. Choose to release harsh memories. (If you continue to poke an injury, scratch a scab, or reopen a wound, it takes much longer to heal. This is not to suggest that you totally blot out your history; just don't *live* in the past.) Focus on what is going *right* in your life. Look for your blessings.

_____ •Due to an inability to concentrate, you may show a diminished capacity to think clearly or make firm decisions. Your ability to process information, reason, and communicate, are also at risk, as is your creativity.

_____ •Expect your memory to be impacted by the constant stress involved. You may be unable to recall important aspects of events, or the order in which they occurred, or you may block them out totally. With your brain suddenly having a Black Hole effect, it's important to keep a journal or log or calendar, to help you remember. You may recall shards of memory at odd moments, causing you to revise your original reports. As a result, your listeners may think that you are "making things up." Recognize that both are normal responses.

_____ •Listen to your hunches. Pay attention to your body messages. Trust your gut responses. Your inner self knows when you are in the presence of danger. Do not disregard your personal, built-in alarm system. It is a survival skill. Do not deny or ignore these warning signs, simply because you've never relied on them before. Trust and respect your inner safety signals. This is not the time to be giving the benefit of the doubt, or second chances.

_____ •Stand up for your rights. Speak up for what you need, want, and deserve.

_____ •When dealing with rude law enforcement clerks or disinterested police personnel, do not blush and stammer about. If anyone says (or shows) that you are not a priority, this is not the time to hold your thoughts, in an effort to appear soft, sweet, and gentle, or civilized and mannerly. (You can get your point across by being assertive rather than aggressive.) Just determine that you will not to be bulldozed. Learn to act in your own self-interest. Stiffen your backbone. Do not leave without satisfaction! Remind yourself that you are not dealing with storm troopers or the KGB.

_____ •Chronic stress is considered to be biologically toxic to your brain. Experts tell us that the human brain cannot endure prolonged stress without producing a negative biological response. Trust in the ultimate justice of the Universe, and let go of poisonous thinking: self-pity, resentment, bitterness, and victimhood.

_____ •Understand that in order to nurture your brain effectively, you must nurture your body and emotions, too.

_____ •Recognition is central to recovery. Determine to face your fears. Experience the crud, the muck, and the mire, the violence and dysfunction. Then let it go. It is important to release negative experiences by refusing to dwell on them. Get past it. Find a reason to move forward and rebuild your life.

_____ •Live a conscious life. Accept your situation as it is. Embrace yourself as you are. Seek help as needed. Determine to make some changes.

_____ •Regularly praise yourself for your courage and the progress you've made toward your safety goals. Celebrate your small day-to-day victories.

_____ •This is not the time for a second-rate performance. Don't settle for mediocrity, or aspire to simply be competent or average. You need to ratchet up your own expectations. Put your hands on the steering wheel of your life. Be a purposeful thinker with a clear goal in mind: *survival.*

EMOTIONAL HEALTH

_____ •You are responsible for your own emotional health. As the pressure can become unbelievably tense when dealing with a stalker or abuser, commit to making extreme self-care a top priority.

_____ •Understand that victims who attempt to resist assaults suffer far less psychological harm than those who simply make no effort at all to defend themselves. Determine to fight back in whatever way possible.

_____ •Stalking and abuse lays a heavy psychological burden on the victim's shoulders, whose emotions are analogous to those of a hostage. Substantial emotional distress is apparent. Understand that struggles over your own issues of trust, safety, and intimacy are normal, as are bouts of anxiety, rage, personal depression, and recurring symptoms of trauma. Resolve not to buckle under pressure.

_____ •Know that you may experience "down" or "blue" periods for an extended length of time, accompanied with crying spells, for seemingly no reason that you can see. There is ample reason. Believe it. Determine that you're experiencing an emotional break*through* not a breakdown. Know that healing begins with the repair of your emotional injuries.

_____ •Allow yourself to go through all five stages of grief: denial, anger, bargaining, grieving, and acceptance. Feel your emotions fully.

_____ •Know that self-nurturance is a form of protection and defense. Move from self-neglect to self-care, unconditional self-love, and acceptance. Give yourself some attention. Identify what you need to do to take care of yourself, and tend to your own needs. Give yourself some TLC. Understand that even the smallest bit of gentleness with yourself will have an immediate beneficial impact. Make time for some first-class indulgences. Pamper yourself.

_____ •Experts tell us that it takes between 200 to 240 days to break the *strongest* combat veteran. Understand that sustained terror has the same result, no matter what its source. Consider the length of your personal trauma. Know that the longer your trauma lasted, the deeper the emotional wounds, the more symptoms are involved, and the slower your recovery.

_____ •Survivors of domestic battery, child abuse, stalking, rape, and combat, share the same psychological syndrome: post-traumatic stress disorder ("shell shock"). Read the research. Know what to expect. An estimated 5 percent of Americans—more than 13 million people—have PDST. You are not alone.

_____ •If your stalking situation is the result of a prior abusive relationship, understand that the verbal and emotional abuse you endured can be more damaging in the long run than the physical abuse. Seek help.

_____ •In such cases where a partner became an abuser or a stalker, it is paramount to remember that you are not at fault: You didn't want this, you didn't encourage this, nor did you ask for any of this to happen. Deception, half truths, and outright lies limited your foresight. You were blinded by mistaken identity. It is not your fault.

_____ •Realize that stalking and abuse victims tend to mistrust their own judgment upon meeting new people, often becoming overly suspicious of other's motives and objectives. This negative reaction makes it difficult to form *any* new relationship, whether of a casual, personal, or professional nature. Fight the impulse to see everyone in the same light, and to paint everyone with the same brush. It will only further isolate you.

_____ •Being on the receiving end of a stalking experience may shatter your sense of community. You may consider it easier to withdraw from society than to deal with your distrust, suspicion, and cynicism. Expect a feeling of disconnection from others, and realize that it is one-sided. Guard against those thoughts. Isolation does not help your situation.

_____ •Build a circle of emotional protection around you: family, friends, neighbors, stalking survivors. Join a support group. Have a telephone buddy. Get individual counseling, as needed. Constant companionship and reassurance is important. Do what you have to do to take care of yourself emotionally.

_____ •You may experience a significant feeling of detachment, a loss of interest in your former passions and activities. Keep active. Work to fill your days with people, places, and things. Don't despair. Know that you *will* regain the world you thought you'd lost. You will eventually find a renewed sense of life, purpose, and meaning. It's just a matter of time.

_____ •Expect that you may experience a numbness of emotions, leading to intimate and/or sexual problems in other relationships. Your ability to both give and receive love will be impacted, and you may worry about your ability to ever love again. Understand that this, too, shall pass.

_____ •Pay close attention to how you talk to yourself (*It's too hard; I'm too tired; It's not going to help anyway; I'll never get away; There are too many obstacles; Nobody cares*, et cetera). Get that *Poor, Poor, Pitiful Me* song out of your head. Banish the voice that whines, "It's not fair! Why me?" You are what you think. Name what is happening, by saying to yourself, "There's that old tape again." Push through your negative patterns. Clear the fog in your head and silence the excuses and distracters. Suspend such self-talk. Attitude is all-important.

_____ •The saying is true: Worry is like a rocking horse; no matter how fast you go, you never get anywhere. Understand that worry is a choice. Realize that worry takes the place of action. You can lessen worrying about your situation by taking stock of where you are, making self-protection plans and/or escape plans, and putting them into action. Just having a method to achieve your goal can break the gloom-and-doom cycle. Actually putting your plan in motion is therapeutic, which will relieve your stress considerably.

_____ •Pay attention to your dreams, and respect them. Keep a notebook (with pen and flashlight), or a tape recorder by your bed, and record your dreams directly upon awakening.

_____ •Immerse yourself in the subject of dreams. Realize that dreams can teach you by connecting your unconscious to your conscious. Contemplate each separate dream meaning, as well as their collective meaning.

_____ •Understand that you may experience reoccurring nightmares of stalking, abuse, or rape events. This is certainly understandable, and expected. Understand that traumatic nightmares—with themes of danger and violence—can revisit you for years.

_____ •Expect flashbacks. Small, seemingly insignificant reminders (a song, a smell, a phrase, a picture, a sound, or an object) can evoke vivid memories, with the same emotional intensity as the original event.

_____ •Sometimes, for no apparent reason, recurring memories of the event will intrude.

_____ •Know that extreme distress may occur simply by driving past the areas in which your stalking or battering experiences once occurred. (I found it difficult to drive through several sections of town, in which such horrible events happened. I boycotted certain places for years, taking alternate routes, and going out of my way, simply because I didn't want to recall such experiences.)

_____ •You may have a distorted perception of your future. You may feel that your life is no longer meaningful or purposeful. Or you may think that you don't even *have* a future (as in, "When he gets me..."). Similarly, you may believe that what little time is left to you will not be normal, or enjoyable in any way whatsoever, because you just seem to be going through the motions. Guard against setting up a self-fulfilling prophecy. Know that your feeling of inner deadness will eventually evaporate.

_____ •There are times when you are going to be *consumed* with anger, feeling bitter and resentful. This is a natural and expected response when dealing with any unfair situation. However, make sure that you aren't lashing out at others. They are not the ones you are *really* mad at. (One afternoon, as I drove into a parking lot, I noticed a woman sitting in her car, idling, directly in front of the drug store doors, facing the wrong direction. I thought she must have been picking up someone. I turned down an aisle, parking in the first slot that was open, quite some distance from the woman. As I exited my car, she got out of her car, and started calling me unpleasant names. She said that I *knew* she wanted that parking space, and that I took it anyway. *Say, what?* She followed me into the store, raving about "her" space. It was clear to me that she was angry with someone else—her husband, boss, or some such—and was displacing her anger onto me. I became a convenient target for letting off steam.) Do not displace your anger.

_____ •Because of your heightened levels of stress, constantly being on edge, and your diminished tolerance, your are prone to over-react at the slightest provocation. Count to ten before you say or do something damaging.

_____ •Do not misdirect your anger at yourself either. Guard against your rage becoming self-destructive.

_____ •Know that a preoccupation with suicide—both thoughts and attempts—is reported in the research, concerning those who have been on the receiving end of either childhood trauma, abusive relationships, rape, stalking, or combat. Do you fit in one or more of these categories? Then know that you may be at risk, and that this tendency is an *expected* byproduct of having been in such a terrifying situation. Don't give power to those ideas. Let those thoughts drift on by without agitating about them. Don't feel shocked or guilty or embarrassed about having such intruding, unexpected thoughts. Determine to broach the subject with trained professionals. Talk it out, work it out, with someone.

_____ •Realize that suicide does not represent the only way out, it is simply *one* way out. Don't direct your unexpressed hatred against yourself. Don't let your stalker or abuser win by default. Do not give him/her the satisfaction of knowing that you *will* be together—at least in his/her thoughts—for all eternity. Fight that inclination.

_____ •Understand that a revenge fantasy is simply a momentary wish to rid yourself of the memory of your trauma. The desire for retaliation is normal, and does not mean that you are bad, or that you have taken on the qualities of your stalker, batterer, or rapist, or that you have sunk to the same level. Don't beat yourself up over this. It is simply a way of mentally coping, a form of catharsis, a way of restoring your sense of power. Eventually, you'll recognize that no revenge can *ever* compensate for the damage done to you, and you'll come to terms with getting even. You'll get past this, with your fantasy falling by the wayside, which will free you to pursue justice in other ways. (Know, however, that an all-consuming focus on vengeance is one of the most toxic emotional poisons to your biological system, causing major dysfunctions.) In time, you'll learn from personal experience, that the old adage is true: Living well is the best revenge.

_____ •Know that getting help is a sign of strength.

_____ •As a survivor, you may want to focus your energies to help others in similar circumstances. In your personal life—on a one-to-one basis—you may raise hope and awareness through the simple retelling of your story. Or you may want to transcend your experience by undertaking a wider and more formal approach through some sort of social action: legal, educational, political, or religious. It is a way to claim your power, and reconnect with your community. You can become an individual activist—at your own time and pace—or participate with others in a collective, organized, show of strength and shared purpose, or both.

_____ •Understand that Post-Traumatic Stress Disorder symptoms are subject to return when you're under stress, or meeting new challenges, or are reaching new milestones. Experts say that recovery is never complete. It is an ongoing struggle. Issues and symptoms are likely to recur throughout your life. Know that the more knowledge and understanding you have about PTSD, and related syndromes, the less the impact. Visit pdstalliance.org for more information and help.

_____ •Do not allow fear to rule your days. Emphasize the positive. Expect things to improve. Work toward upgrading the quality of your life. Make the most of each day. Celebrate being alive.

_____ •Realize that a component of psychological health is someone who has a good sense of humor about practically anything. When you become exhausted with reality, you need a time-out. Find something to laugh about on a daily basis, even if it's just a silly sitcom show.

_____ •As ever, hope for the best, as you prepare for the worst, and determine to never give up, and never give in.

SUPPORT SERVICES SAFETY

_____ •If you have a stalker or abuser, it is your responsibility to gain as much information and knowledge about such behavior, as possible. This is not the time for the proverbial "ostrich/head in the sand" approach, or to shrink from the subject, or procrastinate about taking care of yourself. That will only prolong matters, allowing them to escalate. The situation will not go away of its own accord. Do your homework. Commit to finding what support services are available in your area. Information is now available in many forms: books, videos,magazines, journals, newspapers, TV, movies, speeches, and the Internet.

_____ •Understand, however, that stalking behavior research is in its infancy— an early stage of development—so some studies may seem at odds with others. As such, don't let doubt get in the way. Keep researching the material.

_____ •Recognize that an abuser's or stalker's attitudes, perceptions, and emotions toward you are liable to change over time. So don't get complacent, thinking you have him/her all figured out, as infatuation can quickly spiral down into vindictiveness. Expect a change in behavior. Be on the lookout for it.

_____ •Realize that the police, law enforcement agencies, and the criminal justice system are reactive—getting into the fray *after* the fact—whereas you need a proactive effort. You must make the first move.

_____ •Reach out to others for their help. Look for experts in the field. You really need a personal professional on your side—such as a victim assistance advocate, a consultant, or a lawyer—to guide you through the system, and make it work for you. Consider those you might want in your corner, and pursue their participation. Get experienced input. (At a loss as to how to find a consultant, I asked at both a commercial site that sells equipment for fishing and hunting and a shooting range, for recommendations. As a result, I hired a retired policeman, to give me input and advice.)

_____ •If money is not a concern, consider engaging the services of a private investigator, a bodyguard, or a private security firm.

_____ •Reach out to mental health professionals for their support. Contact individual stalking, abuse, rape, or kidnapped survivors who have had similar experiences. Their stories can provide you with much needed inspiration ("If they could do it, so can I"), suggestions ("Why didn't I think of that?"), and support ("I'm not alone"). Join a group that specializes in lending a helping hand in time of need. If you are not ready for face-to-face contact yet, check the Internet for such survivor groups and information.

_____ •Whatever your belief system, incorporate the ecclesiastical into your daily life. Attend your local church, synagogue, temple, or mosque. Take time to renew your spirit. Practicing your religion can give you meaning in times of despair. Research shows that those who are religiously active have more hope, greater optimism, and have a greater protective effect.

_____ •Religious institutions have an enormous potential to benefit society by speaking out—with conviction, support, and compassion—on such issues as domestic abuse, stalking, and rape. Suggest such programs at your place of worship.

_____ •Idealism is what we strive for, while realism is how we actually conduct our daily lives. Both have their benefits and liabilities. Along with the self-help books you are reading, take time to read books of a spiritual nature, for a sense of balance.

_____ •Pray. It doesn't matter if you address your prayers to God, to any divine being, an energy force, or the Universe at large. Prayer requires no special skills, particular words, or specific form. Just pray in whatever way you can, spontaneously from the heart. Hundreds of studies show that prayer has a positive affect, mentally, emotionally, and physically, whether you are an atheist, agnostic, or true believer.

_____ •Develop close personal relationships with specific law enforcement personnel—substation police, detectives, D.A.s, prison officials, parole officers—in the various cities involved. (In my case, I kept in contact with specific individuals in three local cities: the one I lived in, the one my stalker lived in, and the one in which I worked, in addition to the state parole agency.) The sooner you get others involved, the sooner you can prevent violence, or at least minimize the likelihood of harm. Know that a good working relationship and communication will lead agencies to provide a significant level of response.

_____ •Understand, however, that your endangerment can be increased due to police inaction or inappropriate action. Therefore, if proper information or support is not readily forthcoming, get your local elected officials involved. Do not be afraid to approach them. They work for *you*. (I sought, and received, help and suggestions from two city politicians.)

_____ •Unfortunately, since only *two* percent of the women who are raped will ever see their rapist go to jail, experts suggest that you ask your detective or chief of police the following questions: (1) "Has my rape test been tested?" (2) "Have the results been entered into the state and national databank?" Usually, it is a money situation that causes the city or county to backlog their rape kits. Make waves.

_____ •Local newspapers can also support your efforts, by printing your story, and showing how it affects others. (It has been my experience that the more publicity you have, the more elected officials and law enforcement will *want* to help, and the faster that help will spring into action.)

RECOVERY

In a society that avoids looking outside the range of normal experience—where pain is ignored, and unpleasantness of any kind is sanitized, or quickly forgotten—no one wants to see it, think about it, or deal with it. Few people consider the after effects of a vicious mugging or rape, beyond the obvious physical problems. Few people know how debilitating a stalking experience can be, what with the continual expectation of danger, the general anxiety, the ongoing exhaustion, the unpredictability of the situation, the intense fear, the relentless emotional strain, and the intermittent violence, not to mention the uncertain chance of actual survival. The constant threat takes a heavy toll on one's quality of life. Most fail to recognize the long-term impact of encountering such negativity; the damaging psychological effects.

Whether it was a single overwhelming event (an attack or rape), repeated abuse (incest, physical or sexual violence), or prolonged stalking, you can expect to find a variety of reactions among your family, friends, coworkers, and acquaintances. There are some that flat out won't believe your tale of woe, as the behavior described is too bizarre to even consider, while others find the whole situation too horrible to even contemplate. Some will question your word, simply because you can't remember everything in *exact* chronological order or in *precise* detail (having no knowledge of episodic amnesia, repression, dissociation, and the like, nor the understanding that *one* remembered episode stands for many). And then there are those, who, barely concealing their disbelief or criticism, contend that you are overreacting or overdramatizing; that you are obviously exaggerating or embroidering the events. (One man's comment to me: "Well, your stalker can't be very *good* at it, since you're still alive." How sensitive. Besides the obvious—I'm still here because of good defensive measures and a lot of luck—he didn't grasp the fact that the longer one is stalked, the higher the risk of violence. And it's not over yet.)

There are others who will judgmentally assume that *you* caused the problem and brought the whole experience upon yourself; that something about you attracted the stalker's attention and you *encouraged* the fixation, as in "What did you do to lead him on?" or "What did you do to provoke him?" They feel that somehow you are at fault for putting yourself at risk, not realizing that stalking originates only in the *mind* of the stalker, not in your appearance or your behavior. (Another man challenged me on this point, when I was giving a speech. His total Cause and Effect philosophy didn't allow for the randomness of a stalker's choice of a victim. Agitated, he just wouldn't let the subject drop, and became loud and argumentative. Some in the audience booed him, while others invited him—in no uncertain terms—to sit down and shut up. Some people even tried to escort him out of the room, while others apologized for his reaction. I sensed that something else was going on, and quietly told him that I would talk with him after my presentation. He was immediately silent, and I was able to finish the speech without further ado. Sensing that the man was in torment, I spoke with him in private, whereupon he broke down. He confessed that his sister had a stalker, and he was having a hard time dealing with this shattering experience. He couldn't come to terms with his inability to help, nor the disconnect with his own worldview, and his now shaky foundation of faith. In a sense, he, too, had lost his sense of self. It was easier to blame the victim. Proving, yet again, that it is not only the victim that is traumatized; but family, friends, and society, as well.)

In the case of domestic violence, there are some that will consider you a masochist, asking you, in an accusing tone, "How could you have let this happen? Why didn't you just *leave*?" (having no knowledge of research showing that victims of domestic abuse leave an average of *eight* times before successfully disengaging entirely; that often, the stalking is so horrendous that victims return to their partners as a way to survive and protect their families). As a result, many onlookers will have little empathy or compassion for your painful experiences.

Finally, there may even be a smaller, more suspicious group that accuses you of ulterior motives. Some feel that you are simply looking for undue sympathy. Others see you as actively courting publicity, characterizing your story as a public relations stunt, or a calculated move, at best. A further few will even accuse you of outright lying.

Know that it's more convenient for them *not* to believe you, than to consider the individual, social, and educational ramifications of the situation. It's safer to remain neutral, than to take a side in this moral dilemma. It's less stressful to just throw up their hands and do nothing, than to take action. Settling for an easy answer, they ignore the wider implications, never considering how their inactions are likely to effect others in the long run. They ignore the opportunity to benefit the wider community.

You need to rise above such negative and hostile responses. Do not let these unknowing and small-minded people further damage your dignity and debase your self-esteem. Do not give them the opportunity to heap further dishonor upon you. In essence, you are being victimized all over again. Chalk up their responses to ignorance and insensitivity. Don't let them compound the damage. Expect it and ignore it. Comfort yourself with the knowledge that if they had to spend even one day in your situation, they'd understand your position immediately. Sift through your feelings and get past their petty reasoning. Release, detach, and let it go.

Know that your recovery cannot occur in isolation. In the aftermath of *any* extreme event—stalking, combat, rape, incest, battering, kidnapping—close personal support is important. Connect to those with whom you feel safe and who give you recognition, support, and reassurance; those who are loving and caring; those who are willing to provide listening ears and warm hugs, along with emotional support. This is not the time for strangers, unless you have no one else.

Weeks afterward, you may want to talk it out with an individual therapist, skilled in the particular trauma you have experienced. Months, or years later, you may feel the need to connect with others—a twelve-step program, a survivor group, or an interpersonal psychotherapy group—who have endured similar experiences, and have a depth of understanding that normal society lacks. The shared experience can be an important resource in recovery: sharing information, fostering strengths and coping abilities, tips on self-care, self-protection, and the like. Such groups are powerful (Vietnam Veterans say that such groups are the *only* support that truly understands), and can lessen your feelings of distrust and isolation. With acceptance, compassion, and tolerance, groups appear to be the most effective of all sources of help.

Mental health experts say that if a relationship is dead, you need to bury it, which is exceeding hard to do when your stalker or abuser won't let go. Even so, experts encourage you to tell all, and get it out of your system. Make a conscious decision to explore your mind and your heart: face the facts, face your fears, and face the music. Connect all the dots. Rise above denial, accept the truth about yourself, your past, and certain circumstances, and look at reality head on. It is *essential* to your mental and emotional health that you mourn your losses and tell your story. Specialists agree that the telling of your trauma is considered to be imperative in your recovery process. Your personal testimony becomes a *gift* to others, which is considered to be an important aspect of healing.

See your life as a challenge, not a tragedy. Look for the growth pattern. Find the lesson in your experiences. Look at the positive side of your trauma. What have you learned? Do you now make your own choices and decisions? Do you stand up for yourself? Do you have more confidence in your abilities? Do you have a firmer grip on your ability to face *anything*? Is it easier to encounter difficulties, and overcome challenges? Do you have a deeper sense of gratitude? Do you appreciate the beauty in your life? Do you have fewer illusions? Do you now know what is most important to you? Have you strengthened your personal relationships? Do you think differently? Have you improved the way in which you handle some things? Do you use setbacks to solidify your commitment? Do you appreciate humor, even in your darkest hours? Is there a sense of fun and laughter in your life? Do you have a greater sense of empowerment? Do you have a life of direction and purpose? Do you feel mentally or emotionally stronger? Take pride in your *courage*, and the fact that you've survived. Celebrate each and every one of your days.

It is well known in clinical circles that survivors of extreme situations who *successfully* recover, are those who refuse to be silent on the issues, who take some form of action, and who demand social change. Your speaking out can be a service to others. Take the risk in order to benefit the wider world. You may want to devote yourself to the various issues of stalking, or you may strive for justice, becoming an activist, of sorts. In any case, you will be enlarging the circle of understanding to this increasing societal problem. Friends and relatives may provide you with much needed advice, support, and assistance, as well as loving care, and affection, but that is *all* they can offer. You must discover your own power. You must bring about your own recovery. Live a full, productive, meaningful life, in spite of your trauma. Commit to moving forward.

STAGES OF RECOVERY*

Stage One: safety, basic care, one day at a time

Stage Two: focuses on the traumatic events, tells story to a trusted few, mourns, comes to terms with the past

Stage Three: reveals secrets to others, accuses perpetrator, challenges the indifference of bystanders, reintegration, interpersonal relationships, reconnection with normal everyday life, looks toward future, creates a survivor mission

*Judith Lewis Herman, *Trauma and Recovery: The Aftermath of Violence— From Domestic Abuse to Political Terror.* New York: Basic Books, 1992, 217-218.

Refuse
to be a
victim.

PART III

LAWS RELATED TO STALKING

The first anti-stalking law in the United States was passed in California in 1990. The Violence Against Women Act of 1994 brought about a major change in the national attitude toward both domestic violence and stalking. California's stalking law was revised at that time, and other associated stalking provisions and statutes were enacted. There are now specific stalking laws in all fifty states, as well as the District of Columbia, although there is some variation from state-to-state. Canada, the United Kingdom, Australia, and New Zealand quickly followed suit, with similar laws considered and/or enacted in Europe and parts of Asia.

STALKING LAW

"Any person who willfully, maliciously, and repeatedly follows or harasses another person and who makes a credible threat with the intent to place that person in reasonable fear for his or her safety, or the safety of his or her immediate family, is guilty of the crime of stalking."

(CA Penal Code Section 646.9)

RELATED STALKING LAWS

It is a crime for any person who is convicted of stalking (felony or misdemeanor) to possess or have custody or control of a firearm.

(CA Penal Code Sections 12021 (a) (1) and (c) (1))

The victim can sue the stalker for general, special, and punitive damages.

(CA Civil Code Section 1708.7)

The victim can obtain a civil restraining order at no cost.

(CA Code of Civil Procedure Section 527)

A stalking victim's employer can obtain a restraining order.

(CA Code of Civil Procedure Section 527.8)

A stalking victim may request confidentiality regarding DMV records.
(CA Vehicle Code Section 1808.21)

TERRORIST THREATS

"Any person who willfully threatens to commit a crime which will result in death or great bodily injury to another person, with the specific intent that the statement be taken as a threat, even if there is no intent of actually carrying it out, which, on its face and under the circumstances in which it is made is so unequivocal, unconditional, immediate, and specific as to convey to the person threatened a gravity of purpose and an immediate prospect of execution of the threat, and thereby causes that person reasonably to be in sustained fear for his or her own safety or for his or her immediate family's safety."
(CA Penal Code Section 422)

THE TARASOFF DECISION

This California Supreme Court decision holds that "The protective privilege ends where public peril begins." It rules that clinicians are obliged to use reasonable care to *protect* the intended victim of a patient's violence, which may at times include the warning of the victim.
(Tarasoff v. Board of Regents, 1976)

FEDERAL STALKING LAWS

Stalking laws at the federal level were enacted making it illegal to stalk across state lines, with specific punishment guidelines.

Violent Crime and Law Enforcement Control Act of 1994
This federal law opens up FBI records to civil as well as criminal courts for use in domestic violence cases.
(Title IV, Subtitle F, Sections 40601-40611)

The Interstate Stalking Punishment and Prevention Act of 1996

This act makes it a crime to cross over the state line to stalk someone. It carries a penalty of five years in prison, which increases to years in those cases involving serious injury or the use of a weapon, to 20 years for permanent disfigurement or a life-threatening injury, and to life in prison for those incidents that end in the victim's death. (Unlike some state antistalking laws, the stalker doesn't have to commit an act of violence, or be a spouse for former intimate partner, nor does the victim have to have a restraining order against the stalker to press charges.)

(Title 18 USC Section 2261)

RELATED FEDERAL LAW

WEAPONS LAW OF 1996

Congress passed a law saying that anyone who is convicted of domestic violence (felony or misdemeanor) is prohibited from owning, carrying, or transporting a gun. (The law hasn't yet figured out how this applies to police officers and military personnel who are guilty of domestic violence, since it interferes with their ability to make a living.

Refuse
to be a
victim.

RECOMMENDED READING

STALKING

Allen, J.G., *Coping with Trauma: A Guide to Self-Understanding* (American Psychiatric Press, 1995).

Barnhill, John & Rosen, R.K., *Why Am I Still So Afraid? Understanding Post-Traumatic Stress Disorder* (Dell, 1999).

Bates, Lyn, *Safety for Stalking Victims: How to Save Your Privacy, Your Sanity, and Your Life* (iUniverse Press, 2001).

Berry, Dawn Bradley, *The Domestic Violence Sourcebook* (Lowell House, 2000).

Boon, Julian & Sheridan, Lorraine (ed), *Stalking and Psychosexual Obsession: Psychological Prospectives for Prevention, Policing, and Treatment* (Wiley, John & Sons, 200).

Davenport, Jane, *Exit the Game: For a Stalker-Free Life* (GreatUNpublished, 2001).

Davis, Joseph A. (ed), *Stalking Crimes and Victim Protection: Prevention, Intervention, Threat Assessment and Case Management* (CRC Press, 2001).

Davis, Keith E., Frieze, Irene & Maiuro, Roland (ed), *Stalking: Perspectives on Victims and Perpetrators* (Springer, 2001).

Douglas, John E. & Olshaker, Mark, *Obsession: The FBI's Legendary Profiler Probes the Psyches of Killers, Rapists, and Stalkers, and their Victims and Tells How to Fight Back* (Pocketbooks, 1998).

Dunn, Jennifer L., *Courting Disaster: Intimate Stalking, Culture, and Criminal Justice* (Aldine de Gruyter, 2002).

Gedatus, Gustav Mark, *Stalking: Prospectives on Violence* (Capstone Press, 2000).

Goodale, Renee, *Stalking and Harassment: Ending the Silence That Kills*, 2nd ed. (Survivors of Stalking, Inc., 1996)

Gross, Linden, *Surviving a Stalker: Everything You Need to Know to Keep Yourself Safe* (Marlowe & Company, 2000).

Hardy, Bo. *Defensive Living, When Defensive Driving, Diets and Exercise Aren't Enough to Keep You Alive and Well* (Defensive Living Press, 1992).

Herman, Judith Lewis, *Trauma and Recovery: The Aftermath of Violence—From Domestic Abuse to Political Terror* (Basic Books, 1992).

Lardner Jr., George, *The Stalking of Kristin: A Father Investigates the Murder of His Daughter* (The Atlantic Monthly Press, 1995).

Meloy, J. Reid (ed), *The Psychology of Stalking: Clinical and Forensic Perspectives* (Academic Press, 1998).
_____ *Violence Risk and Threat Assessment: A Practical Guide for Mental Health and Criminal Justice* (Specialized Training Services, 2000).

McCann, Joseph T., *Stalking in Children and Adolescents: The Primative Bond* (American Psychological Association, 2001).

Mullen, Paul E., Pathe, Michele & Purcell, Rosemary, *Stalkers and Their Victims* (Cambridge University Press, 2000).

Orion, Doreen, *I Know You Really Love Me: A Psychiatrist's Account of Stalking and Obsessive Love* (Dell, 1997).

Pathe, Michele, *Surviving Stalking* (Cambridge University Press, 2002).

Schaum, Melita & Parrish, Karen, *Stalked: Breaking the Silence on the Crime of Stalking in America* (Pocket Books, 1995).

Scott, Michael, *How to Lose Anyone Anywhere: The Stalking Victim's Roadmap to Safety* (Stealth, 1996).

Snow, Robert L., *Stopping a Stalker: A Cop's Guide to Making the System Work for You* (Plenum, 1998).

Spence-Diehl, Emily, *Stalking: A Handbook for Victims* (Learning Publications, Inc., 1999).

Wright, Cynthia, *Everything You Need to Know about Dealing with Stalking* (Rosen Publishing Group, 2000)

PERSONAL SAFETY

Aftab, Parry, *The Parent's Guide to Protecting Your Children in Cyberspace* (McGraw Hill, 2000).

Ayoob, Massad, *The Truth About Self-Protection* (Police Bookshelf, 1983).

Caignon, Denise & Groves, Gail, *Her Wits About Her: A Collection of Women's Self-Defense Success Stories* (HarperCollins, 1987).

Danylewich, Paul Henry, *Fearless: The Complete Personal Safety Guide for Women* (University of Toronto Press, 2000).

De Becker, Gavin, *The Gift of Fear: Survival Signals That Protect Us From Violence* (Little, Brown, 1997).
_____ *Protecting the Gift: Keeping Children and Teenagers Safe (and Parents Sane)* (Dell, 1999).

Givens, Beth and the Privacy Rights Clearinghouse, *The Privacy Rights Clearinghouse* (Avon, 1997).

Grover, Jim, *Street Smarts, Firearms, and Personal Security: Jim Grover's Guide to Staying Alive and Avoiding Crime in the Real World* (Paladin Press, 2000).

Hardy, Bo, *Defensive Living: When Defensive Driving, Diets, and Exercise Aren't Enough to Keep You Alife and Well!* (Defensive Living Press, 1992).

Hayes, Gila May, *Effective Defense: the Woman, the Plan, the Gun* (Firearms Academy of Seattle, 1994).

Kurr, Stephan, *How to Bodyguard Yourself: A Personal Protection Guide for Women* (Booklocker.com, Inc., 2002).

Langelan, Martha J., Garner, Hugh & MacKinnon, Catharine A., *Back Off! How to Confront and Stop Sexual Harassment and Harassers* (New York: Fireside, 1993).

Livingstone, Neil C., *Protect Yourself in an Uncertain World: A Comprehensive Handbook for Your Personal and Business Security* (MasterMedia, 1996).

Lovette, Ed & Spaulding, Dave, *Defensive Living: Attitudes, Tactics, and Proper Handgun Use to Secure Your Personal Well-Being* (Looseleaf Law Publications, 2000).

Luna, J.J., *How to be Invisible* (St. Martin's Press, 2000).

McCaughey, Martha, *Real Knockouts: The Physical Feminism of Women's Self-Defense* (University Press, 1997).

Quigley, Paxton, *Not An Easy Target: Self-Protection for Women* (Fireside, 1995).

Rich, Curt, *Drive to Survive!* (MBI, 1998).

Snortland, Ellen, Beauty *Bites the Beast: Awakening the Warrior Within Women and Girls* (Lightning Source, 2001).

Turner, Marie, *The Woman's Safety Handbook* (PageFree Publications, Inc., 2001).

FIREARMS

Ayoob, Massad F., *In the Gravest Extreme: The Role of the Firearm in Personal Protection* (Police Bookshelf, 1980).
_____ *Aboob Files: The Book* (Police Bookshelf, 2002).
_____ *Gunproof Your Children* (Police Bookshelf, 1986).

Bijlefeld, Marjolijin, *People For and Against Gun Control: A Biographical Reference* (Greenwood, 1999).

Branca, Andrew F., *The Law of Self-Defense: A Guide for the Armed Citizen* (Operon Security, 1988).

Homsher, Deborah, *Women and Guns: Politics and the Culture of Firearms in America* (Sharpe, Inc., 2002)

Kleck, Gary, *Point Blank: Guns and Violence in America* (Aldine de Gruyter, 1991).

Lott Jr., John R., *More Guns, Less Crime: Understanding Crime and Gun-Control Laws*, 2nd ed. (The University of Chicago Press, 2000).
_____*The Bias Against Guns: Why Almost Everything You've Heard About Gun Control is Wrong* (Regnery Publishing, 2003).

May-Hayes, Gila, *Effective Defense: The Woman, the Plan, the Gun* (Police Bookshelf, 1994).

Nisbet, Lee (ed), *The Gun Control Debate: You Decide* (Prometheus Books, 2000).

Poe, Richard, *The Seven Myths of Gun Control: Reclaiming the Truth About Guns, Crime, and the Second Amendment* (Crown Publishing Group, 2001).

Quigley, Paxton, *Armed and Female* (St. Martin's Paperbacks, 1989).

Snyder, Jeff, *A Nation of Cowards: Essays on the Ethics of Gun Control* (Accurate Press, 2001).

Stange, Mary Zeiss & Oyster, Carol, *Gun Women: Firearms and Feminism in Contemporary America* (Fast Track Books, 2000).

Waters, Robert, *The Best Defense: True Stories of Intended Victims, Who Defended Themselves With a Firearm* (Cumberland House, 1998).

RELATED INTERNET WEBSITES AND LINKS

Hundreds of useful links are listed through the following sites:

STALKING

ABCNEWS.com: 20/20: Stalking on the Internet

Angels in Blue Stalking Tutorial

Antistalking

Antistalking Website—www.antistalking.com

Are you being stalked? Tips for protection

AWARE—www.aware.org

Burglary

Cyberangels—www.cyberangels.org

www.demographics.com/Publictions/AD/98-ad/9803-ad/ad980311.htm

www.feelsafeagain.org

How to Lose Anyone Anywhere

Institute for Law and Justice—www.ilj.org/stalking/

Love Me Not—www.lovemenot.org/default2.htm

Model Antistalking Code for the States—
    www.ojp.usdoj.gov/ocpa/94Guides/DomViol/appendb.htm

National Center for Victims of Crime—www.nvc.org/law/statestk.htm

National Crime Victimization Survey

National Victim Center safety tips—www.nvc.org/gdir/svsafety.htm

Prevalence and Health Consequences of Stalking

SafetyEd Cyberstalking Information

www.smalltime.com/notvictims/stalking.html

www.ssa.gov

www.ss.ca.gov/safeathome

Stalkers

Stalking—www.ilj.org/stalking/factinf.htm

The Stalking Assistance Site—www.stalkingassistance.com

Stalking Awareness Network—stalkingawareness.org

Stalking Behavior—www.stalkingbehavior.com

Stalking FAQ—www.madcapps.com/Writings/faqabout.htm

Stalking in America: Findings From the National Violence Against Women Survey

Stalking in Cyberspace—www.ilj.org/stalking/cyberspace.htm

Stalking Resources on the Internet

Stalking Survivors' Sanctuary and Solutions—www.stalkingvictims.com

Study of the Effectiveness of State Antistalking Efforts and Legislation

Survivors of Stalking (SOS)—www.soshelp.org

www.uic.edu/depts/safetynet/stalking.html

Vandalism

Violence Against Women Stalking Information

Working to Halt Online Abuse

SEXUAL ASSAULT

Arming Women Against Rape and Endangerment (AWARE)—www.aware.org

Center for the Protection of Sexual and Domestic Abuse—www.cpsdv.org
  Feminist Majority—www.feminist.org/911/assaultlinks.html

MaleSurvivor—www.malesurvivor.org

www.rape101.com

Rape, Abuse & Incest National Network—www.rainn.org

Sexual Assault Information Pages—
  www.cs.utk.edu/%7Ebartley/saInfoPage.html

DOMESTIC ABUSE

American Bar Association—Commission on Domestic Violence

Arming Women Against Rape and Endangerment (AWARE)—www.aware.org

Artemis—www.survivorsofdv.website-works.com

Center for the Prevention of Sexual and Domestic Abuse—www.cpsdv.org

Cybergrrl SafetyNet—www.cybergrrl.com/views/dv/index.shtml

Family Violence Prevention Fund—http://endabuse.org

Feminist Majority—www.feministorg/911/crisis.html

Los Angeles Commission on Assaults Against Women (LACAAW)—
  www.lacaaw.org

National Center for Victims of Crime—www.ncvc.org

National Coalition Against Domestic Violence—wwwncadv.org

National Network to End Domestic Violence—www.nnedv.org

National Organization for Victim Assistance—www.try-nova.org

National Organization for Women—www.now.org/issues/violence/index.html

Paladin Group—Domestic Violence—www.silcom.com/~paladin/madv

Phenomenal Women of the Web—Against Domestic Violence—
     www.phenomenalwomen.com/help

Safe Horizon—www.feminist.org/911/crisis.html

Silent Witness National Initiative—www.silentwitness.net/

Transforming Communities

Women Against Domestic Violence (WADV)—www.wadv.org/support.htm

www.ssa.gov

Violence Against Women Act (VAWA)

Violence Against Women Office—www.ojp.usdoj.gov/vawo

PERSONAL SAFETY

American Civil Liberties Union (ACLU)—www.aclu.org/privacy/

The American Women's Self Defense Association—www.awsda.org

Assault Prevention Information Network

www.autoguide.net/schools/driving.shtml

Axis Intervention & Training

Arming Women Against Rape and Endangerment (AWARE)—www.aware.org

American Women's Self-Defense Association (AWSDA)

www.ayoob.com/cat1.html

www.backgroundchecks.com

Christina Nealson's Home Page—www.christinanealson.com

www.consumer.gov/idtheft

CyberAngels—www.cyberangels.org

CyberGuards—www.cyberguards.com

David Baldwin's Trauma Pages—www.trauma-pages.com

www.defendyourself.net

www.defensedevices.com
    Domestic Violence

www.epic.org/privacy/consumer/legal.html

Federal Bureau of Investigation

Fierce and Female video series—www.dr-ruthless.com/frameset.htm

www.FindLaw.com

www.firstinc.com

Gavin DeBecker, Inc.—www.gdbinc.com

Impact/Model Mugging—www.impactboston.com/about.htm

www.jlusa.com

www.junkbusters.com

Los Angeles Commission on Assaults Against Women(LACAAW)—
www.lacaw.org

Melissa Soalt's self-defense videos—www.dr-ruthless.com/frameset.htm

National Center for Post Traumatic Stress Disorder Information—
www.dartmouth.edu/dms/ptsd

National Victim Center—www.nvc.org

National Women's Martial Arts Federation—www.nwmaf.org

No Nonsense Self-Defense

National Violence Against Women (NVAW)—www.wadv.org/support.htm

www.nsc.org/training/index.cfm

Office of Community Oriented Policing Services

Office for Victims of Crime—www.ojp.usdoj.gov/ovc/

Paxton Quigley—www.paxtonquigley.com

Personal Protection

Privacy Rights Clearinghouse—www.privacyrights.org
www.ptsdalliance.org

www.racesearch.com/resources/drvschls.html

Rape Agression Defense (RAD)—www.rad-systems.com

Refuse to Be a Victim

Scotti School of Defensive Driving—www.ssdd.com

Self-Defense: A Basic Human Right

Sexual Assault Information Page

Sourcebook of Criminal Justice Statistics

Victim Assistance On-Line—www.vaonline.org

Violence Against Women Office—www.ojp.usdoj.gov/vawo

Web Detective—Find People

www.whoishe.com

www.whoisshe.com

Women Halting Online Abuse (WHOA)

CHILDREN'S SAFETY

Amber Alert

www.childfindofamerica.org

Childhelp USA—childhelpusa.com

Children Are Worth Saving (CAWS)—www.geocities.com/Capitol Hill/7836

www.crimeproofing.com

The Eddie Eagle Gun Safe Program

www.find-missing-children.org

www.getnetwise.org

Girls and Boys Town—girlsandboystown.com

Impact Model Mugging: Children's Classes—
     www.impactboston.com/children.htm

www.kidscentralstation.com

Megan's Law

www.missingkids.com

National Center for Missing and Exploited Children

www.prevent-abuse-now.com

Safekids.com

SafeTeens.com

Scooters Child Gun Safety Info-Center

www.thekidsafenetwork.com

www.unitedcareusa.org

www.yoursafechild.com

FIREARMS

Anti-Gun Mom Turned Survivor

Armed Females of America

Gun Owners of America

Mothers Arms

National Rifle Association

NRA's Women on Target

NRA Women's Pages

Paxton Quigley—www.paxtonquigley.com

Second Amendment Sisters—www.2asisters.org
Self Defense for Women Magazine—www.sdwmag.com/about.asp

Women&Guns Magazine—www.womenandguns.com

Women and Guns in the News

Women's Firearm Network

Women, Minorities and Guns

Women To Arms—www.womentoarms.net

Women's Voice

FIREARMS SCHOOLS

Arming Women Against Rape and Endangerment (AWARE)—www.aware.org

www.ayoob.com

www.firearmsacademy.com

www.frontsight.com/home.htm

www.gunhoo.com

www.insighttrining.com/ps/main/about.htm

www.martialartsresource.com/firearms.htm

www.nrahq.org/education/index.asp

www.optionsforpersonalsecurity.com

wwwpaxtonquigley.com

www.sigarmsacademy.com

www.smith-wesson.com/acd/new.htm

www.thunderranchinc.com

www.weaponstraining.com

MAPS & DIRECTIONS

www.expedia.com

www.mapquest.com

www.vicinity.com/geocities/driving.html

0-595-28879-0

www.ingramcontent.com/pod-product-compliance
Lightning Source LLC
Chambersburg PA
CBHW061302280526
45784CB00002B/867